THE AIREDALE WAY

A 50-mile walk
from Leeds to Malham Tarn

by

Douglas Cossar

Published by the Ramblers' Association (West Riding Area)

Other publications by the Ramblers' Association (West Riding Area)

Ilkley Moor map & guide
Ramblers' Leeds
Washburn Valley map & guide
Family Rambles around Bradford
Dales Way Handbook (with the Dales Way Association, annually)
Kiddiwalks (new edition Spring 1995)

The Airedale Way first published 1996

© Douglas Cossar 1996

All rights reserved.
No reproduction permitted without
the prior permission of the publishers:

RAMBLERS' ASSOCIATION (WEST RIDING AREA)
27 Cookridge Avenue, Leeds LS16 7NA

ISBN 0 900613 95 5

Cover photograph: The River Aire at Gargrave

Printed by Duffield Printers, Leeds

Publishers' Note
At the time of publication all footpaths used in these walks were designated as public rights of way or permissive footpaths, but it should be borne in mind that diversion orders may be made from time to time. Although every care has been taken in the preparation of this guide, neither the author nor the publisher can accept responsibility for those who stray from the routes described.

Contents

Author's Note

Stage 1 Leeds to Shipley

1.1   Leeds Station to Horsforth 9
1.2   Horsforth to Apperley Bridge 13
1.3   Apperley Bridge to Shipley 15

Stage 2 Shipley to Steeton

2.1   Shipley to Bingley. 19
2.2   Bingley to Keighley. 23
2.3   Keighley to Steeton. 29
       Circular Walk from Cross Hills to the
       Cowling Pinnacles and Ickornshaw 33

Stage 3 Steeton to Gargrave

3.1   Steeton to Cononley 37
       Circular Walk from Kildwick to the Jubilee Tower 41
       Circular Walk from Cononley to Lothersdale. 43
3.2   Cononley to Skipton 47
       Circular Walk from Low Bradley 51
       Circular Walk through Carleton Glen 53
       Circular Walk from Skipton to Sharp Haw 55
3.3   Skipton to Gargrave 59

Stage 4 Gargrave to Malham Tarn

4.1   Gargrave to Airton 63
4.2   Airton to Malham Tarn 67

Down River to Woodlesford and Castleford. 71
Useful addresses 75
Record of walks completed 76

The Ramblers' Association

What do we do?

- We work non-stop to protect footpaths.
- We campaign for more freedom of access to mountain, moorland, woodland and other open country.
- We defend the beauty and diversity of Britain's countryside.

Sixty years of successful lobbying at local and national level have been entirely dependent on membership subscriptions, donations and legacies.

We are a registered charity with over 120,000 members working hard to promote the health and educational benefits of walking in the countryside.

The **West Riding Area** is one of the 51 Areas of the Ramblers' Association which cover England, Wales and Scotland. It includes the whole of West Yorkshire and parts of North Yorkshire around Selby, York, Harrogate, Ripon, Skipton and Settle, as well as the southern part of the Yorkshire Dales National Park. The Area has nearly 4,000 members and is divided into 13 Local Groups.

What can you do?

If you use and enjoy the footpath network, please remember what the Ramblers' Association has done to make this possible and help us to protect it, by becoming a member now. For further information write either to

Mrs Dora Tattersall, West Riding Area Membership Secretary, 10 Woodvale Grove, Lidget Green, Bradford BD7 2SL

or The Ramblers' Association, 1/5 Wandsworth Road, London SW8 2XX.

Remember the Country Code:

Guard against all risk of fire.

Take your litter home. As well as being unsightly, it may be a hazard to livestock.

If you find a gate closed, be careful to close it again behind you. If it is open, leave it open.

Do not pollute streams or rivers, ponds, lakes or reservoirs.

Keep dogs under control: they may frighten other walkers or be a threat to livestock.

Protect, wildlife, plants and trees.

Keep to public paths across farmland.

Take special care on country roads.

Use gates and stiles to cross fences, hedges and walls.

Make no unnecessary noise.

Leave livestock, crops and machinery alone.

Enjoy the countryside and respect its life and work.

Author's Note

Those of us who live in Leeds appreciate having "on our doorstep", as we say, the glorious landscapes of the Yorkshire Dales, although few of us would think of walking from the one to the other. But why not? The River Aire, rising amid the spectacular limestone scenery of Upper Malhamdale, on its 88-mile course to join the Ouse near Goole flows through the heart of the city, and provides a natural link route between them. The Airedale Way, by following as far as possible riverside paths, provides easy walking, suitable for all the family.

Why should one walk 50 miles, instead of letting the train, or the bus, or the car take the strain? There is firstly the sheer pleasure of physical exercise, with the added interest of a goal to be achieved, the commitment needed to achieve it and the satisfaction of reaching the end of the walk and knowing that one has got there entirely by one's own efforts. Then one sees much more when one goes on foot, one has time to stop and stare, one develops a closer relationship with the countryside one is passing through. And there is much to be seen in Airedale.

There is the natural world, the different landscapes, the birds and flowers and trees, sometimes in apparently unpromising surroundings (I saw my first kingfisher on the Aire near Bingley), but make no mistake, there is much natural beauty in Airedale, in spite of the closeness of industry. There is history at every turn: the old stone bridges, at least one of them dating from the Middle Ages, the ancient churches, the 17th century farmhouses and halls, the picturesque villages, the mills and all the archaeology of the Industrial Revolution, and the Leeds and Liverpool Canal, which shares the valley with the river as far as Gargrave.

The towpath of the Leeds and Liverpool Canal, built between 1770 and 1816 and with a wealth of natural beauty, fine views and historical interest in its own right, provides indeed another obvious means of access for walkers from the city to the country.

There will be those who will want to walk the Airedale Way in one go, but there will be many more who will collect it bit by bit over a winter or a summer. For them I have divided the route up and made each section (except for the first) into a circular walk. All the walks can be done using public transport, as the railway also shares the Aire valley. The Metro network, with its fare concessions, extends as far as Steeton. The return routes as far as Gargrave make use of the canal towpath, so those who complete the suggested circular walks will also find they have walked the entire canal from Gargrave to Leeds, although I have occasionally included higher level alternatives for those who wish more variety and extensive views.

On each side of the valley there are fine viewpoints, and the Craven countryside between, say, Steeton and Skipton has a wealth of public rights of way and many attractions, which deserve to be better known, so I have included some circular rambles, mainly in this area, off the main route.

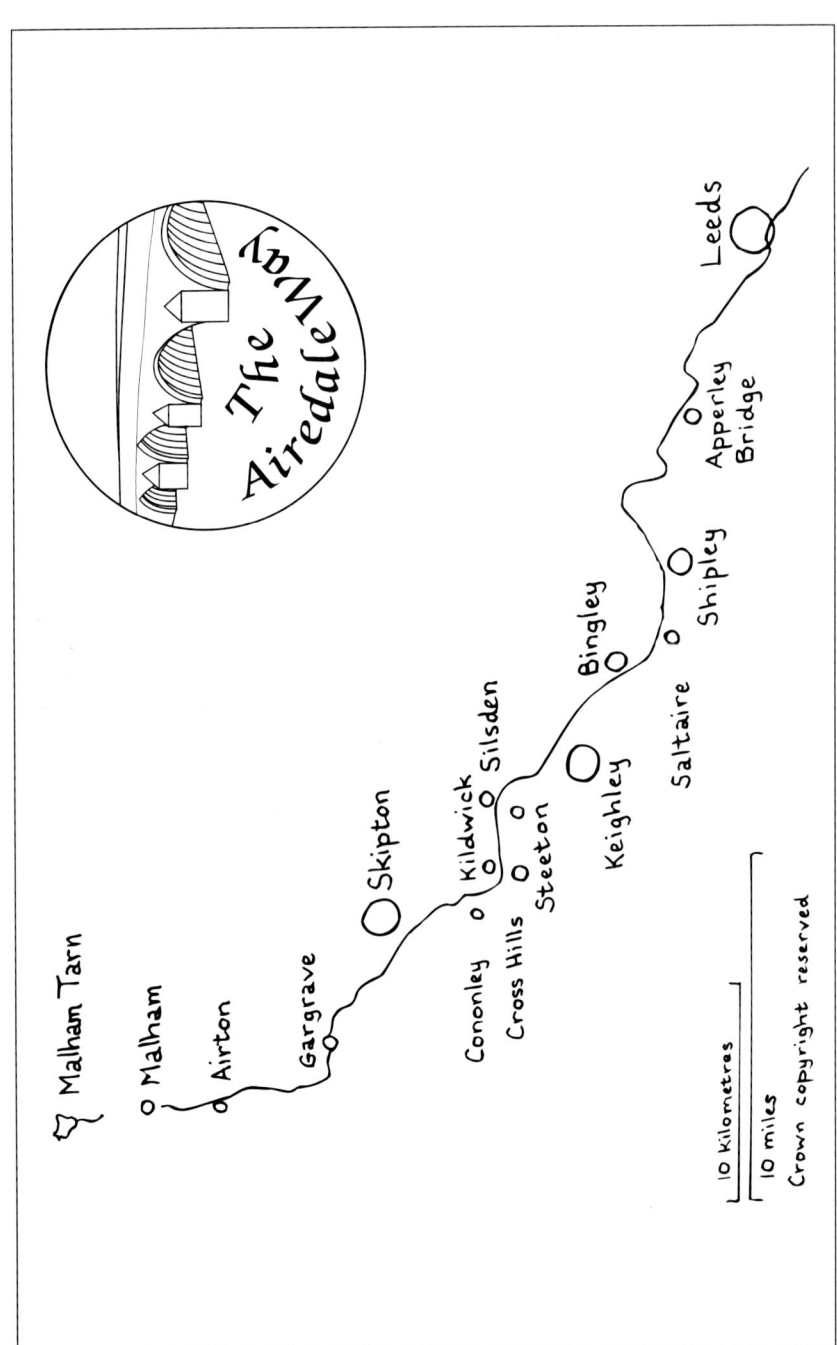

All the paths used are definitive rights of way or permissive paths. I am grateful to the Rights of Way Officers of Leeds and Bradford Metropolitan District Councils and North Yorkshire County Council for their advice and encouragement. I hope that in time the Airedale Way will be signposted and waymarked and become a major recreational asset of our area. If you should come across path problems en route, please report them to the relevant highway authority (their addresses can be found on page 75). Do take particular care crossing railway lines and major roads, and remember to look out for bulls at large in pastures in the summer months, and take suitable evasive action, even if this means a minor trespass. Better safe than sorry!

The Airedale Way logo is based on Kildwick Bridge, and a cloth badge which incorporates it is available from the Ramblers' Association (West Riding Area), 27 Cookridge Avenue, Leeds LS16 7NA price £1.50 plus a stamped addressed envelope.

The route of the Airedale Way can be located on the Ordnance Survey Landranger maps 104 (Leeds, Bradford & Harrogate), 103 (Blackburn & Burnley) and 98 (Wensleydale & Wharfedale). At the start of each walk I have given details of the relevant Pathfinder sheet(s) or Outdoor Leisure maps. The sketch maps which accompany the route descriptions are based on the O.S. Pathfinder maps and are reproduced with the permission of H.M.S.O. They are intended to give an overview of the walks and to supplement the description, but as they are greatly simplified, particularly in built-up areas, they should not be used as a substitute for the description. Distances given on the maps are in kilometres from the start of the Way.

Route directions for the Airedale Way are printed in **bold** in the text, return routes are in ordinary type, matters of interest are printed in *italic*.

Happy walking!

Douglas Cossar
May 1996

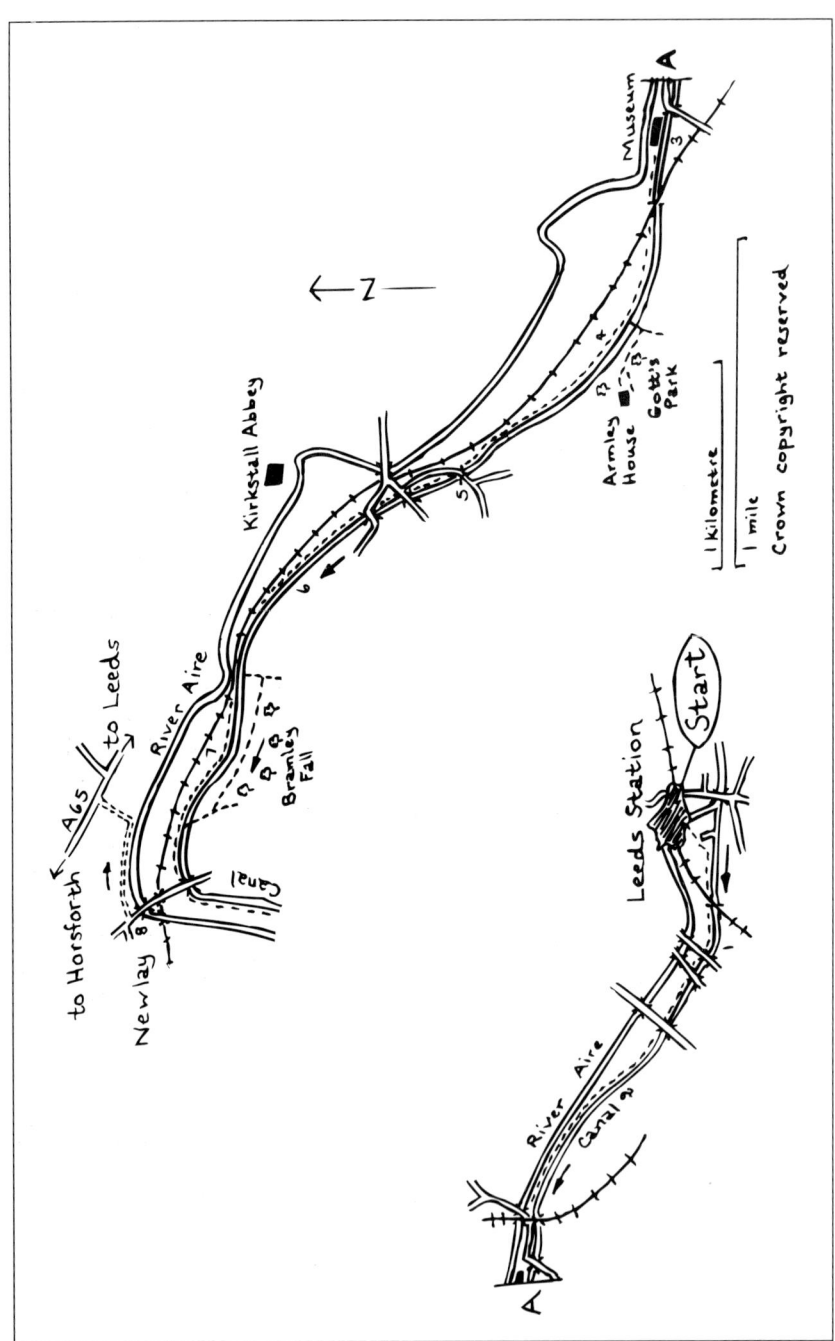

Stage 1 Leeds to Shipley (14 miles, 22.7 km)

This stage can be divided into three shorter walks:
1.1 Leeds Station to Horsforth (5½ miles, 8.75 km linear), returning to Leeds city centre by bus.
1.2 Horsforth to Apperley Bridge (8 miles, 12.8 km) (circular).
1.3 Apperley Bridge to Shipley (10 miles, 16.1 km) (circular).

1.1 Leeds Station to Horsforth

Pathfinder 683 (Leeds). As there is no riverside path from the city centre upstream, this first walk uses the canal towpath as far as Newlay Bridge. Short detours can be made to the Leeds Industrial Museum at Armley Mills and Kirkstall Abbey and the Abbey House Museum. For a detailed guide to the historic sites and buildings along the Aire valley between Leeds and Rodley see "The Leeds Waterfront Heritage Trail" by Peter Brears (Leeds City Museums, 1993). Refreshments are available at the Abbey Inn, Newlay Bridge. The return to the city centre is made by bus 33/732/733/734/735/736 from New Road Side, Horsforth. Cars may be parked by the playing fields near the top of Pollard Lane, off the old Leeds and Bradford Road near Bramley Fall Park, but note that there is no suitable parking lower down.

On emerging from Leeds Station walk straight over the pedestrian crossing to a small white tower building with a sign saying Way Out Bishopgate, go down the steps and turn right to follow the road under the station. Turn right through the arches leading to Granary Wharf and cross the Aire, which flows under the station, then enter the Wharf shopping precinct. Make your way to the car park alongside and turn right along the pavement. At the end of the car park you reach the Leeds Canal Basin. Bear left to the 18th century bridge over the canal with the canal company's original office behind it, but without crossing the bridge keep forward along the towpath, which you follow to bridge 221.

The two 19th century Italianate campaniles on the other side belong to the Tower Works. Bridge 225G is Monk Bridge of 1886, with the city arms incorporated into its ironwork. The next impressive stone bridge with the very large arch and balustrade was built in 1846 for the Leeds and Thirsk Railway. Pass under the bridge, and just after the St.Ann's Ing Lock, on the other side of the canal, are the long low brick railway workshops with the large round-headed windows. The next concrete bridge carries the Inner Ring Road, and when you emerge from it your eye is caught by the large brick Castleton Mill of 1838 with its semi-circular stair tower.

9

Having passed Spring Garden Locks, the massive wall on the other side of the canal is part of the foundations of the 19th century Leeds Forge. The next very striking feature is the Leeds and Thirsk Railway viaduct built in 1846. Continuing, look out for the attractive cast-iron balustrade of the Canal Road Bridge, now on a modern concrete base.

To visit Armley Mills, the Leeds Industrial Museum, which is straight ahead of you after you pass under the Canal Road Bridge, turn right immediately after the bridge through the arch and up the steps, then turn right again to cross the bridge and right again into the museum car park.

Our walk continues along the towpath. The arched stone bridge 225, giving access to the museum, dates from the 1770s. At the end of the high wall enclosing the museum turn right to the viewpoint over the River Aire: the large mill dam is conspicuous, and looking right there is a good view of the museum itself. Pass under the railway bridge, and soon two concrete bridges carry the towpath over the entrances to Power Station Wharf, where barges used to bring the coal for Kirkstall Power Station, but which is now a quiet backwater. The towpath is now quite rural, with the wooded Gott's Park across the canal.

For a detour through the Park, landscaped by Humphrey Repton, to the classical Armley House, once the residence of Benjamin Gott, the owner of Armley Mills, cross the next stone bridge (224) and immediately turn right off the drive, in about 15 yards forking left on a clear climbing path which soon bears right and rises through the woods to a flight of steps. At the top you emerge into the open Park, now occupied by a golf course, and by following the path round the edge of the wood on your right you reach two tarmac paths, either of which will take you to the house, which now serves as the clubhouse for the golf course and also contains a café. Notice the fine views back to the city centre and up the valley to Kirkstall Abbey and beyond. Return by the same route to the canal towpath.

When you reach a bridge preceded by a grassy space with benches and a car park, a detour right to Kirkstall Abbey is possible. Our walk continues along the towpath. The large building on the other side of the canal by the bridge is the former Kirkstall Brewery, from which last century beers were carried down the canal to Goole and exported to Australia and New Zealand. Bridge 221A is the Leeds and Bradford Road Bridge, and after it look right for views of Kirkstall Abbey, the best probably being the one from Kirkstall Lock. Gone now are the extensive rhubarb fields which once dominated this part of the valley. From the three-rise Forge Locks the buildings of Kirkstall Forge, once an important iron foundry, can be seen across the railway and the river. Here too another detour is possible through Bramley Fall, 100 acres of woodland owned by the City Council, an area once extensively quarried: it was from here that the stone came to build Kirkstall Abbey. The woodland paths while attractive are often muddy, and the drier alternative is to remain on the towpath.

If you do decide to make the detour, cross the canal by the top lock and the overflow channel by the footbridge, and ignoring the flight of steps ahead bear right along a clear path. At a fork keep left on the main path which climbs gently through the woods, and at the next fork again keep left to climb some steps to a signpost and a broad cross track. Turn right along this, and walking parallel to the canal below you on the right, follow it all the way to another footpath sign (look out for drier paths to the side of the track which have formed to avoid some of the muddy sections) where another broad track comes in from the left and Newlay Locks are to your right. Keep forward to the locks and re-cross the canal by the lock gate. Resume your journey along the towpath.

At the next stone road bridge (221) fork right to the 18th century Abbey Inn and the charming Newlay Bridge, erected in 1819 and one of the oldest iron bridges in the county. **Cross it. The Airedale Way continues straight up the hill,** but to return to Leeds by bus turn right along the track, cross a stile by a gate (on the right you can glimpse the weir which marks the start of the Kirkstall Forge Goit) and follow the track up to the A65. The bus stop is a short distance to the right.

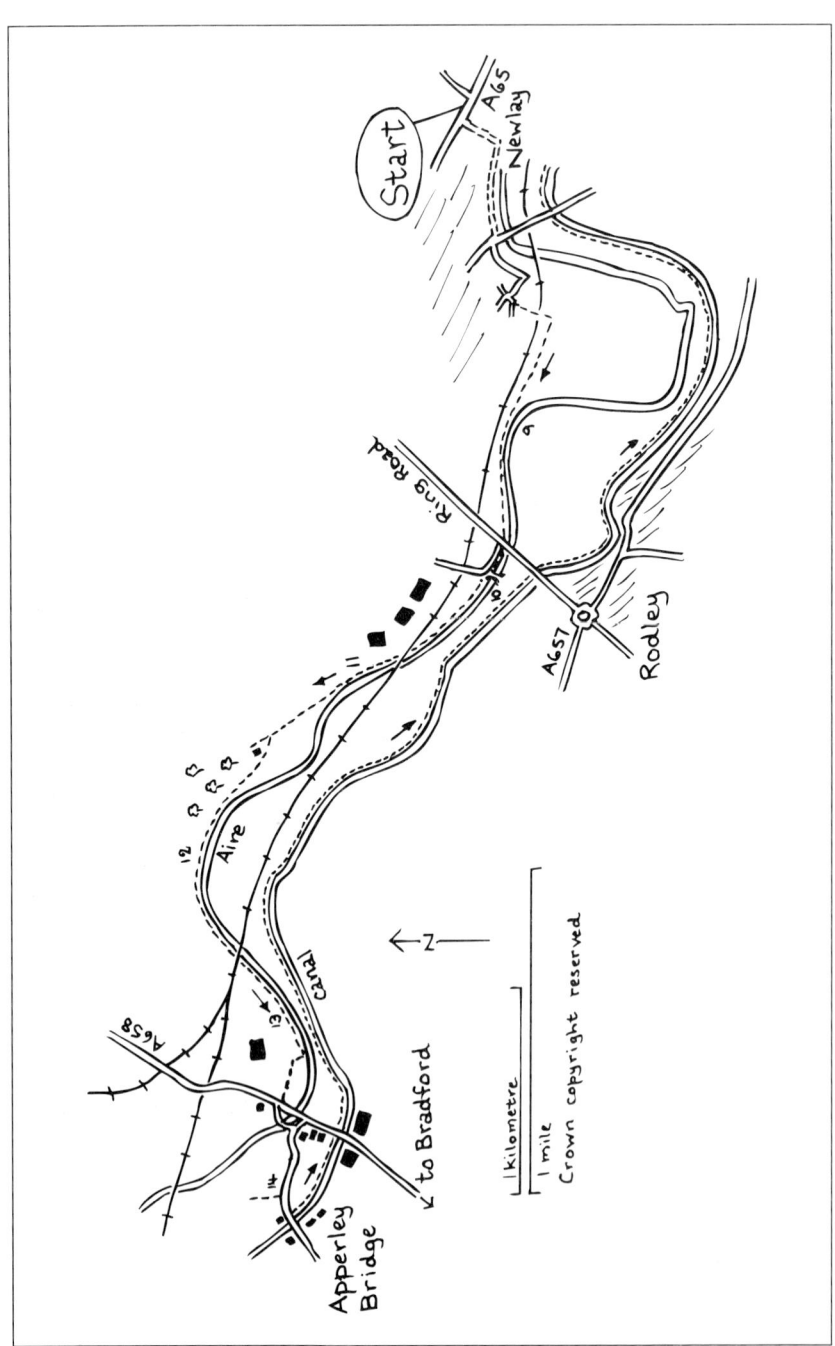

1.2 Horsforth to Apperley Bridge

Pathfinder 683 (Leeds), 682 (Bradford). The start of the walk is reached by taking bus 33/732/733/734/735/736 from Leeds city centre to the junction of Hawksworth Road and New Road Side, Horsforth. At the end of the walk return to the city centre by the same route. Car parking as for the previous walk, or in the car park on the right of the entrance into the Woodhouse Grove School playing fields on Apperley Lane. Refreshments are available at The Abbey Inn, Newlay Bridge, The Railway, Rodley, The Stansfield Arms, Apperley Bridge, The George & Dragon, Apperley Bridge, and on the return route at The Rodley Barge, Rodley.

Having alighted from the bus, walk a short distance in the direction of Horsforth, then turn left down the stony track you used at the end of the previous walk and retrace your steps to Newlay Bridge. Having reached the cross lane with the bollards and the bridge on the left, **turn right up the hill for 50 yards, then turn left along a narrow concrete road. The lane becomes tarmac and soon curves right uphill. Ignore streets forking left off it. Climb to a T-junction and turn left along Newlaithes Road. Where the new houses on the left end, turn left down an unsurfaced track, cross the railway and at the end of the bridge turn right along a fenced path parallel to the railway.** *The view half left is across to Rodley.* **Pass through a stile into the field on the left and keep your direction as before.**

Near the highest point a bench provides a pleasant view up the river to the Leeds Ring Road bridge and beyond it the white chimney of the Sandoz works, which we shall soon be passing. **Drop to a stile and the river bank, for your first experience of walking by the Aire. At forks keep left by the river. Pass under the Ring Road and again keep left at a fork.** *Calverley Lane Picnic Site is up to your right.* **The path soon leads up a few steps to a stile onto an old cobbled lane.** *To the left is the stone Calverley Bridge over the river (built in 1776 after the great flood of that year); crossing it would lead in a few minutes to the Railway Inn at Rodley.*

Cross over the lane to the stile opposite. Pass under a large pylon, and soon you are back near the river, with the Sandoz works to your right. Pass through the barrier at the end of the field and under the railway bridges, then continue on the riverside path. When you reach a wooden fence across the path and the start of a stone wall, Rodley Sewage Works necessitates a short diversion away from the river. So keep the wall on your left, follow it to a track and bear left along this. When you reach an

isolated house, ignore the ascending road ahead and fork left, to pass to the left of the house.

A kissing-gate leads into a fenced path with Cragg Wood to the right. The path soon returns you to the riverside. Eventually a stile in a stone wall leads into playing fields. Keep along the left hand side of these and pass under the railway bridge. There are more playing fields belonging to Woodhouse Grove School, the buildings of which are half right ahead.

Cross another stile in a stone wall and keep forward along the riverside. Pass under the overhead power lines and when you reach a cross wall ignore the stile ahead and turn right. Follow the wall on your left through the playing fields, then turn left along a surfaced path with a fence to your left to the A658 Bradford to Harrogate road. Cross this into Apperley Lane. *A short distance to the right is the Stansfield Arms (the Stansfield family bought Esholt Hall in 1775).* **Cross the Aire by the road bridge** *(another bridge built after the great flood of 1776; it stands on the route of the old coaching road from Manchester, Halifax and Bradford to York, Durham and Newcastle),* **with the George & Dragon ahead** *(a 16th century building, extended in 1704),* **then turn right along Apperley Road.**

Where the road begins to curve left, by a lamppost, a stile in the wall on the right leads down some steps into a field, and this is where the Airedale Way continues.

To return to Horsforth, continue along Apperley Road to the canal and turn left along the towpath. Follow this all the way back to Newlay, where you left the canal on walk 1.1. At Rodley there are two pubs within easy reach, the Railway on the left and the Rodley Barge on the other side of the canal, reached by crossing the swing bridge. Immediately after passing under bridge 221 turn left off the towpath through the barrier and walk down the road past the Abbey Inn, cross the Aire by Newlay Bridge and turn right along the lane which will bring you back to the bus stop and your starting point.

1.3 Apperley Bridge to Shipley

Pathfinder 682 (Bradford), 671 (Keighley & Ilkley). If using public transport, it is simplest to start and finish at Shipley Station, walking the return half of the walk by the canal first, then following the route of the Airedale Way from Apperley Bridge back to Shipley. Cars may be parked in the car park on the right of the entrance to the Woodhouse Grove School sports grounds on Apperley Lane. Esholt village has become a tourist attraction as one of the locations of "Emmerdale Farm". Refreshments are available at The George and Dragon, Apperley Bridge, The Woolpack and Ashwood Tearoom in Esholt, Birdies Tearoom just beyond Esholt and in pubs in Shipley.

From the station forecourt walk down the access road, cross the main road with great care and turn left to pass in front of The Bull Inn. The building to the left of the pub is Killips Carpets and Beds and just beyond it a signposted path leads down to a cast iron footbridge over the canal. This bridge (207D) seems to be known as Gallows Bridge. Cross it and walk forward along the towpath. Bridge no. 208 is an old arched stone one beside a small canal basin. Pass swing bridge no. 209, with the large modern Pace factory across the canal. Just before swing bridge no. 210 the canal is crossed by the Bradford to Ilkley railway.

After a time there is a good view left over the Aire valley to Baildon Church on the hill. After swing bridge 211 there follows an attractive, well-wooded section of the canal. Field Locks is a staircase of three. Around bridge 211B the buildings of Esholt Waste Water Treatment Works are much in evidence. The railway bridge just after swing bridge no. 212 is the line from Leeds to Shipley/Skipton/Carlisle/Lancaster. Dobson Locks with its cottages is an attractive spot. Leave the canal towpath at swing bridge 214, which is where you joined it for the return leg of the previous walk, and turn left along the road. The Airedale Way continues across the stile on the left by the third lamppost along, but remember that refreshment is available a short distance further along this road at the George & Dragon.

Cross the stile and go down the steps, and follow the wooden fence on your left, and where the fence ends pass through a double stile and keep forward up the slope (with a drop to a pond to your right) to cross a stile in the fence ahead. A clear path leads forward through a gap in the old wall ahead. Pass to the left of some more ponds, presumably an old meander of the river, and walk straight across the middle of the field along a clear path to a stile by a gate on the far side. Go through the tunnel under the railway.

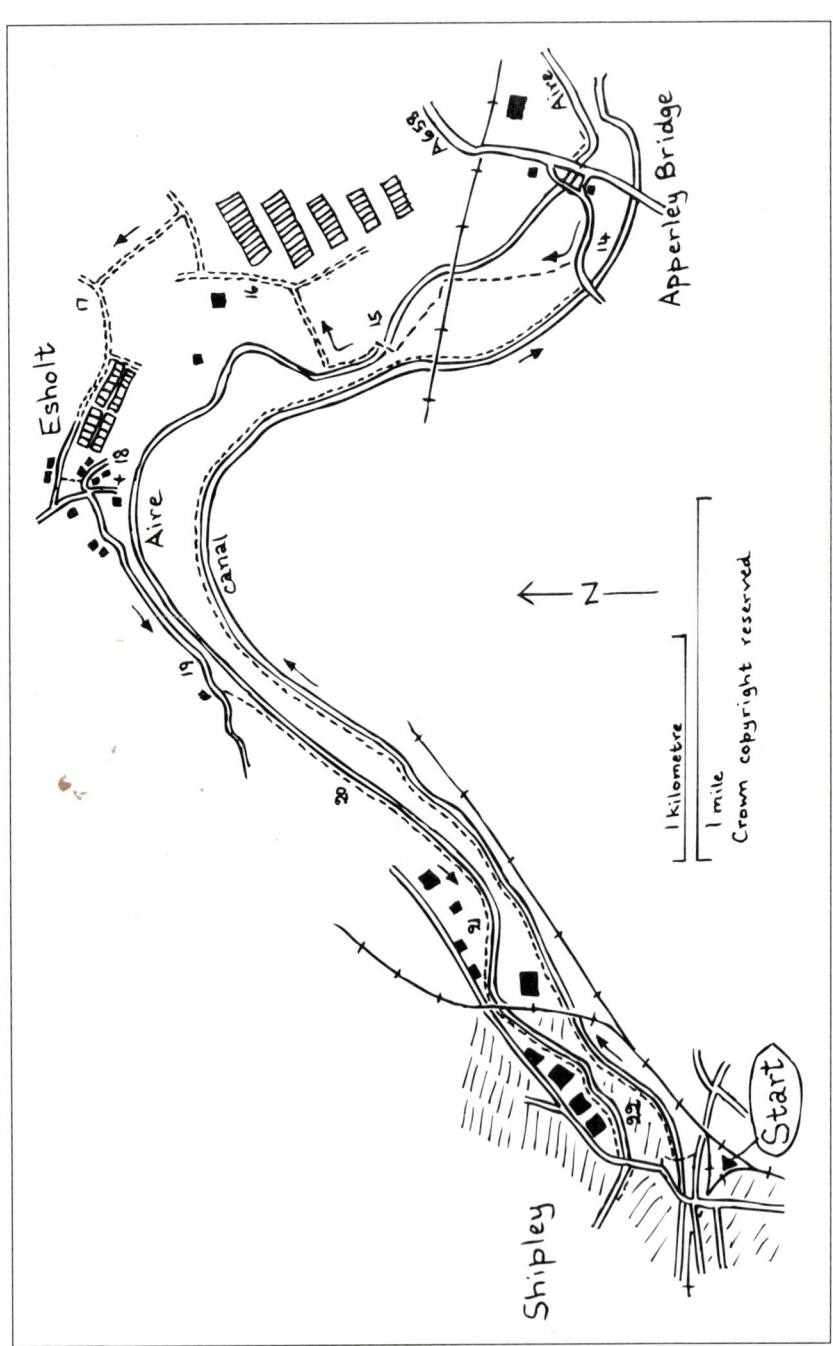

Bear left round the corner of the wall and walk across the middle of the large field, parallel to the river across on the right, to cross a stile in the fence on the far side. Turn right to cross the suspension bridge over the Aire. Turn left parallel to the river, but where the fence on your right turns sharp right, a diversion away from the river is caused by Yorkshire Water's large Esholt Waste Water Treatment Works.

A community of Cistercian nuns was established at Esholt in the 13th century. After the Dissolution of the Monasteries a mansion was built on the site, which was replaced in the early 18th century by Esholt Hall, which in 1775 became the home of the Stansfield family. They sold the estate to Bradford Corporation early this century for use as Bradford's sewage works. So turn right with the fence and follow a track until you join tarmac and pass through a stone gateway. Turn left along the road. Keep straight ahead, ignoring junctions, and pass to the right of the extensive buildings of Esholt Hall Home Farm, some of them now in decay. At the end of the buildings turn right uphill on a narrower road. Near the top there is a view right over a sea of filter beds.

Where the track levels off, near a pumping station on the right, go through a gateway on the left and along another track. On it there is only one junction, where you should ignore a clear track coming in from the right by a large pipe. Pass through a gap by a gate to join the next tarmac road and pass to the right of more filter beds. After they end, the village of Esholt appears down to the left. Near the end of the first group of houses on the right, go through the bollards on the left and walk down a tarmac path into Esholt village, *usually busy with visitors, because this is Emmerdale Farm country, and at the foot of the lane the famous Woolpack Inn and the village centre are on your left.* Turn right, then keep forward along the main road. *Turn left down Church Lane if you want to have a look at the church, Esholt Old Hall and beside it the Ashwood Tearoom and Souvenir Shop.*

Drop down the hill, ignoring Cunliffe Lane on the right, and soon the road has the river directly on its left. Pass Esholt Sports & Leisure Club and the cricket ground. Having crossed a narrow hump-backed bridge you reach Birdies Coffee Shop. Opposite it cross the stile on the left and follow the left hand edge of the field with tall trees (and a rifle range) on your left. At the end of the field cross the stile and keep forward along the riverside path. Cross another stile into a rather narrow riverside path with a hedge to the right and the remains of paving (and lots of tree roots for the unwary to trip over!). Cross straight over a cross path *(the metal bridge over the river was erected in 1889)* and continue by the river.

A kissing-gate leads into a pleasant landscaped area, and just after a bench it is worth making a detour away from the riverside to have a look at it. A few yards further on you could fork right again to reach a stone seat. *By the gate into the works a plate on a stone gives details of this wildife park, inaugurated in 1991. There are benches, and this would be a nice spot for a picnic.* At the far end return to the riverside. The scenery soon becomes more urban as you approach Shipley. Keep on by the river, at length crossing a stone stile. Some way further on there follows a rather unpleasant narrow unprotected section of path, before you pass under the tall viaduct of the Bradford to Ilkley railway line. Now you have ugly factories beside you, and then another narrow unprotected section of path. Climb up some steps to reach a metal footbridge, but ignore it and go down the steps ahead and on along the narrow riverside path. It ends where a tarmac path leads up away from the river.

Follow the high metal fence on your right, walk down a few steps and turn right with the fence. At the first opportunity turn left to pass through some works yards and into a short stretch of fenced footpath. Cross straight over the garage forecourt and turn left at the main road to cross the Aire. The continuation of the Airedale Way is found by crossing the road at the far side of the bridge and descending a few steps onto the riverside path.

To return to Shipley Station, follow the main road for a short distance after the river bridge, then turn left along View Croft Road. At the end of this a ginnel on the right leads up to the canal, and you will recognise that this is where you joined the towpath at the start of the walk. So cross the canal bridge and walk forward to the main road (the Bull is of course a few yards to the left!). Cross the road with care and return to the station.

Stage 2 Shipley to Steeton (11½ miles, 18.5 km)

This stage can be divided into three shorter, circular walks:
2.1   Shipley to Bingley (8 miles, 13 km)
2.2   Bingley to Keighley (8½ miles, 13.8 km)
2.3   Keighley to Steeton (7 miles, 11 km)

2.1 Shipley to Bingley

Pathfinder 682 (Bradford). Start and finish at Shipley Station. There is a pay-and-display car park near Bingley station. A major attraction on the route is the Victorian industrial village of Saltaire, with the David Hockney Art Gallery in Salt's Mill. Guidebooks are available in the village. From Saltaire footpaths lead to Shipley Glen, a well-known beauty spot, and here too the Airedale Way crosses the Bradford-Ilkley Dales Way Link (the Dales Way is a long-distance path from Ilkley to Bowness-on-Windermere). In summer the return to Shipley could be made by waterbus on the canal, a journey of 1½ hours, thus shortening the walk by almost 3½ miles (5½ km). Refreshments are available at The Boat House Inn and various cafés in Saltaire, The Brown Cow, The Old White Horse Inn and various other pubs in Bingley, The Fisherman's, Dowley Gap and pubs in Shipley.

As in the previous walk, from the station forecourt walk down the access road, cross the main road with great care and turn left to pass in front of The Bull Inn. The building to the left of the pub is Killips Carpets and Beds and just beyond it a signposted path leads down to a cast iron footbridge over the canal. Cross it and at the foot of the steps turn left down a ginnel and then left along the next street. Cross the next main road and turn right, then immediately before the bridge over the Aire turn left down a few steps onto the riverside path.

Follow the riverside path until it climbs some steps and joins the canal towpath by the corner of Salt's Mill. Follow the towpath through between the large mill buildings and under the road bridge (no. 207A). *Cross the road bridge to visit Saltaire, where refreshments are available.* **The walk continues by leaving the towpath here through the bollards and walking down past the Boat House Inn and crossing the Aire by the tubular footbridge. Turn sharp left along the first tarmac footpath into Roberts Park and follow it along by the river, passing to the left of the cricket pitch.** *The back view of the statue of Sir Titus Salt can be seen beyond the grass.*

Pass to the left of the cricket pavilion and follow the river past some playing fields and on along the grass. Ignore the next

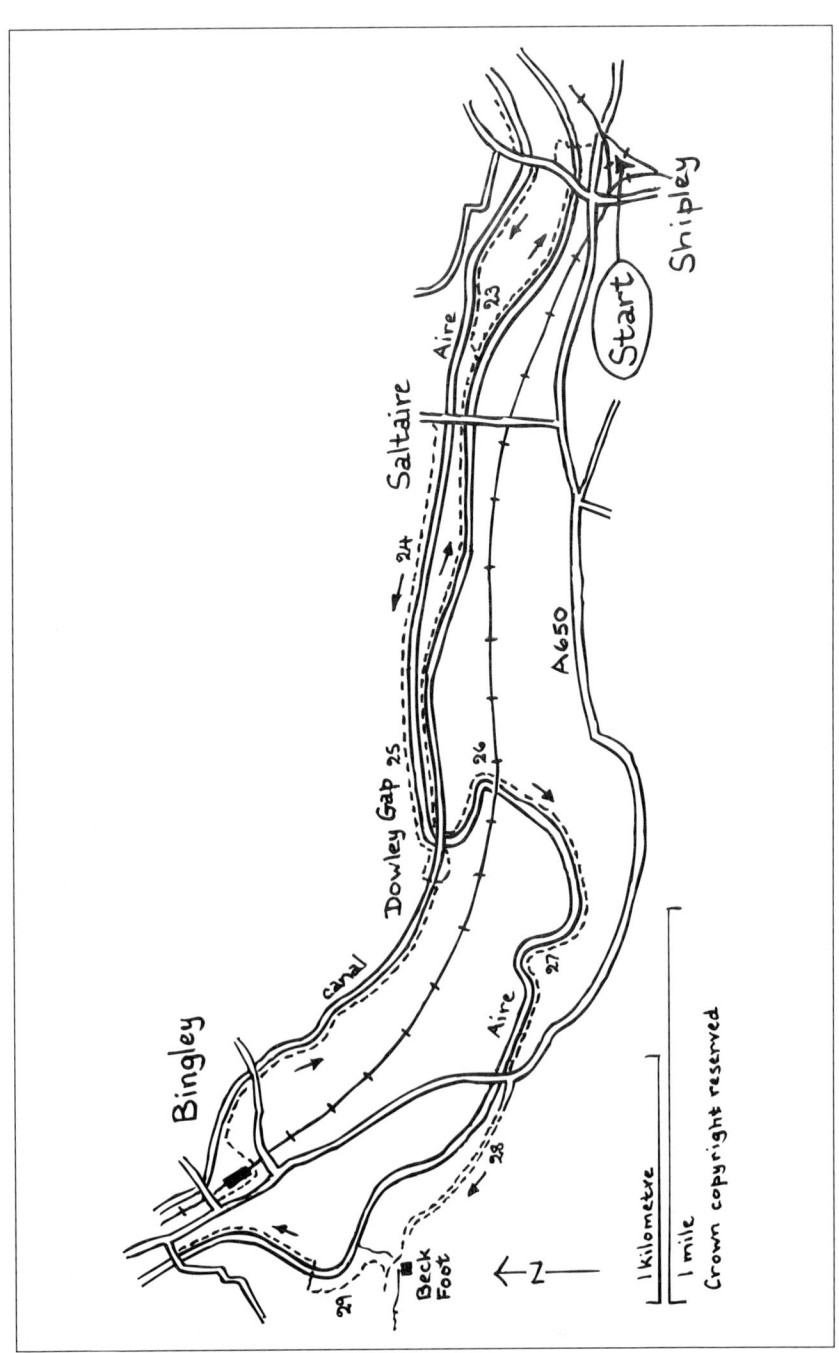

footbridge over the river. *This is where the Bradford-Ilkley Dales Way Link, which has followed the canal towpath from Shipley, crosses the Airedale Way.* **Keep forward to cross Loadpit Beck, which flows down from Shipley Glen, by a footbridge, and join a track. Leave this again after 30 yards by a footpath on the left which passes a weir on the river with a renovated mill on the far side, and to the left of some boathouses, and becomes an attractive wooded riverside path, which is followed all the way until it passes the aqueduct at Dowley Gap, which carries the canal across the Aire, and reaches the towpath again by a stile.**

Turn right along the towpath, which soon crosses to the other side of the canal by an old stone bridge (no.206). Instead of turning right on the other side, leave the towpath again by keeping forward down the track, which soon bears left to pass between filter beds and an old renovated mill, then bends left again and leads back to the aqueduct. Cross this, and after a few yards turn sharp right on a path which drops down the bank and crosses a footbridge. Bear left and follow the path along near the river until you pass under the railway line, pass an entrance into Nab Wood Cemetery, cross a concrete footbridge and continue along the riverside path.

Go through a stile into a walled path and follow this forward until you leave it again through a metal gate. Walk across the field, which you leave through another metal gate. Keep on parallel to the river, passing through some woodland before emerging into another grassy area. Follow the riverside path, passing to the right of playing fields and ignoring a metal bridge over the river but bearing left at it. Enter a fenced riverside path and follow this to the main road (A650) at Cottingley Bridge. Leaving the bridge to your right, cross the main road and walk along Beck Foot Lane opposite. This leads past Shipley Golf Club to Beck Foot Farm, *dating from 1617, but once owned by the Knights of St John of Jerusalem,* **and an arched packhorse bridge** *(built in 1723)* **over Harden Beck.**

Cross the bridge and go through the stile on the right. The path leads across the field towards the fence on the right, then bears left to climb to the right of two old trees and a house and pass through a gap-stile. Walk along the top edge of the wood, then follow the path as it bears right down through the wood. At the foot, descend a few steps and walk across the field to the footbridge over the Aire *(erected for the Festival of Britain in 1951)* **into Myrtle Park. Turn left and walk parallel to the river, soon**

joining a made path. *This is Bingley's attractive "Riverside Walk". To visit the centre of Bingley, with its old Market Hall, Butter Cross and stocks, climb the second flight of steps on the right, leading to an iron archway (not the first one with the wooden handrail by the picnic tables). Bingley was granted its market charter by King John in 1212, but like several other of the Airedale towns it was only in the second half of the last century that it grew from a village into an industrial town.* **Otherwise follow the river all the way to a new housing development** *(look out on the way for a few steps on the right leading to a stile, which gives access to the Ailsa Well, which takes its name from Alice Hird who used to live nearby; the water was unusually hard and thought to be excellent for cooking vegetables)* **and pass through this, under an archway, to reach the B6429 at Ireland Bridge** *(built in 1685).* **The Airedale Way turns left over the bridge,** *(where there is also Timothy Taylor's Brown Cow)* but to return to Shipley turn right past the 17th-century Old White Horse Inn to the traffic lights.

Turn right along Main Street as far as Dryden Street, cross the main road by the pedestrian crossing and continue along Main Street to the next traffic lights where you cross Park Road and then turn left down it. (Keep straight on down over the railway bridge, then turn left for the terminus of the Waterbus.) Take the first right, Wellington Street, pass Bingley Station and continue to the junction with Waterloo Road, cross this and turn right to the next junction, then left down to the car park. A gap in the wall on the far side of this gives access to the canal towpath. Turn right along it.

Just before bridge 205 there is a Waterbus stop and here too is the Fisherman's pub. Then come Dowley Gap locks. At the next bridge (206) (we've been here before!) the towpath changes sides. Cross the aqueduct again, this time on the other side. A pleasant stretch now follows, with the Aire down to the left and Hirst Wood on the opposite bank of the canal. Just before swing bridge 207 there is a Waterbus stop. Follow the towpath through Saltaire to Shipley. Leave the canal at bridge 207D, which is where you crossed it at the start of the walk; cross the bridge and walk up to the main road, which you cross to return to the station.

2.2 Bingley to Keighley

Pathfinder 682 (Bradford), 671 (Keighley & Ilkley). Start and finish at Bingley Station. There is a pay-and-display car park nearby. Scenically this section of the Way is surprisingly attractive, although it does leave the riverside. Keighley is the terminus of the privately owned Keighley and Worth Valley Railway, which runs steam trains to Haworth and Oxenhope, and Cliffe Castle Museum has displays on the geology and natural history of the Aire valley. The major attractions on the return are the National Trust's East Riddlesden Hall, a mansion built by a rich merchant-clothier in the mid-17th century, then the Bingley Five Rise and Three Rise Locks on the canal. Refreshments are available in Bingley, at Robbo's, The Shoulder of Mutton and The Bridge Inn on the outskirts of Keighley and at The Marquis of Granby, Riddlesden.

From the main entrance to Bingley Station turn right, then left at the next junction, then at the traffic lights right along Main Street, crossing it by the next pedestrian crossing. Continue to the next lights, then turn left by the Old White Horse Inn down Millgate and cross the Aire.

Immediately after crossing the Aire bridge turn right into Ireland Street, then in a few yards right again, and in a few more yards left, with the river over the wall to your right. The track soon passes through woodland, then rises slightly away from the river. When you reach the first house, Ravenroyd, bear right through the gateway and follow the track round to the right of the house, through the yard, ignoring a track dropping right towards the river, and on out the other side. Follow the track to the next house, Cophurst, and pass to the left of it to a gate. The track continues with a wood to the left. Pass through a gateway and ignore a path forking half right. Pass through the next gateway at the end of the wood and soon you are joined by another track coming from the left. Go through the small kissing-gate beside the next gate: *the historic settlement of Marley is to your right; the Hall was built in 1627.*

Cross the stile a yard or two to the left of the next gate, turn left, then left again before the next house, on an ascending track with fine views back. You pass two houses before the track leads to a stile by a gate from which a clear path continues uphill through sparsely wooded heather, bilberry and bracken. Keep right at a fork (the left hand branch heads for a wall on the left) and right again at the next fork on a narrower path towards a gate and wall. Cross the stile in the wall corner and follow the wall on the left along until you meet a facing fence: go left through the gateway and then out by a kissing-gate onto a farm access road.

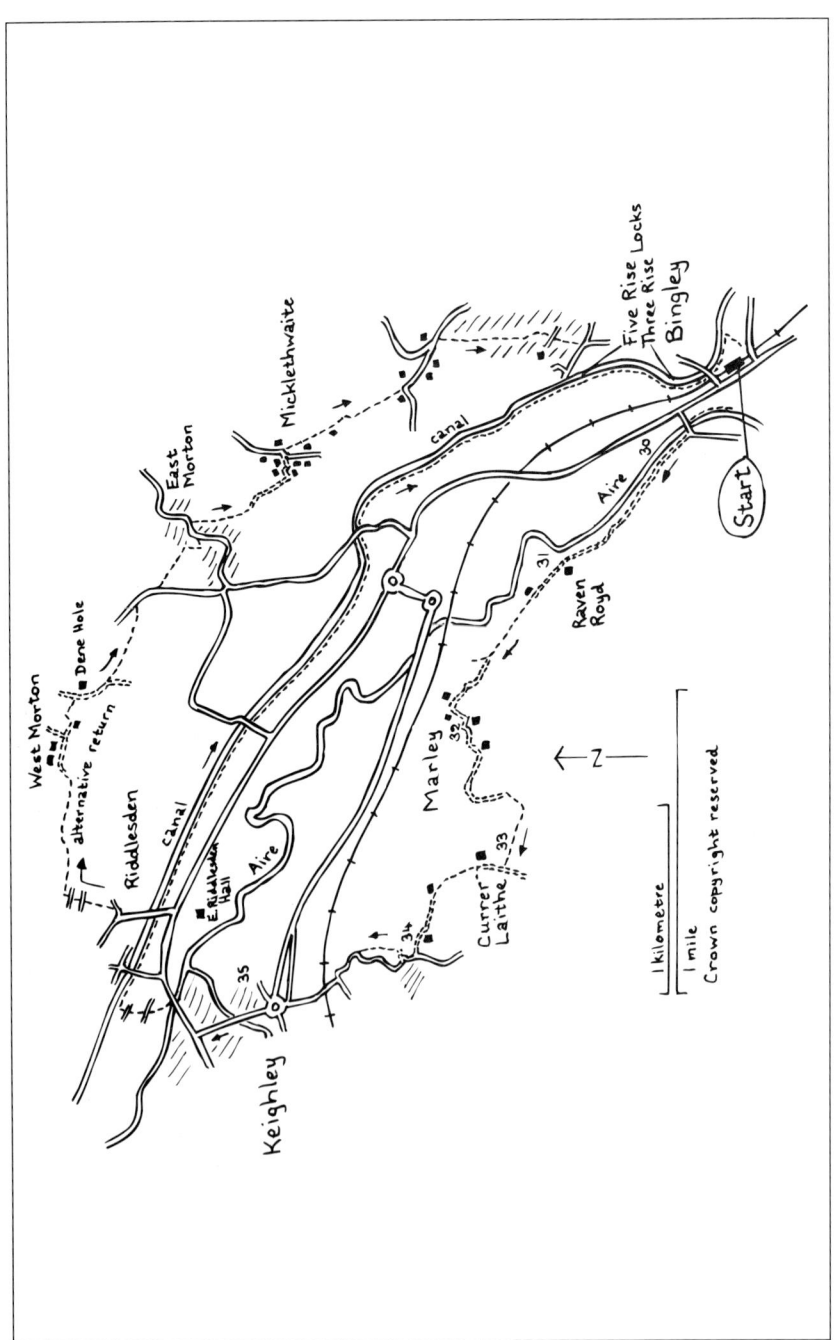

Turn right down the track to Currer Laithe Farm *(the Currers used to be an important family hereabouts)*, **cross the plank bridge beside the cattle-grid and fork left to follow the wall on the left up to a stile in the field corner (ignore a stile in the wall just before this), then keep on by the wall on your left** *(East Riddlesden Hall is visible across the valley)* **to a stile above Jackfields Farm, from which a short section of enclosed path leads to another stile into a field. Keep by the wall on the right to the farm access road and keep forward along this. Pass another farm and reach a motor road by a bus turning circle. Turn right downhill, passing a children's playground which has benches and flat walls to sit on.**

The road curves sharply left. You ought to be able to take the next track off it on the right, which leads to a walled path on the left just before the gate beside the house, but this is at present impassable, so keep on down the road. Go right at a T-junction *(there are two pubs here: Robbo's on the right and The Shoulder of Mutton on the left)* **and at the next junction ignore Valley Road and keep straight on down past the school to the large roundabout. Pass anti-clockwise round this, crossing the dual carriageway and then Marland Road, which leads down to playing fields, and take the next road on the right leading off the roundabout, to the right of the AireWorth Veterinary Centre. You cross the River Worth, which you can hear but scarcely see. At the T-junction turn right, then cross this road by the pedestrian crossing. Continue past the Bridge Inn, and to continue the Airedale Way immediately before the bridge over the Aire turn left down some steps on a signposted footpath.**

To return to Bingley cross the bridge, then immediately turn left down more steps on another signposted path, which leads through a yard between sheds. Then bear right up the track, cross straight over the next street and follow the ginnel opposite up to the canal towpath. Turn right along it.

At swing bridge 197A a very short detour to the right brings you to the National Trust's East Riddlesden Hall. Here too is the start of a higher level return to Bingley. If you do not wish to take it, simply keep on along the towpath to swing bridge 200 at Bingley Five-Rise Locks, where the alternative route rejoins the towpath. To take the alternative, cross the canal, pass The Marquis of Granby and walk straight up the road, Granby Lane. Where the main road swings left at the top, go right for a few yards then take the cobbled path and steps on the left just before the No Through Road sign. Cross two streets on the stiff pull up, pass in front of Barley Cote Cottages, up more steps and then the path turns right and passes through a stile into a broader way, which leads to a stile by a gate.

Keep along by the wall on the left, which curves left to a stile by a gate. Bear right, now with the wall to your right. Cross the stile ahead, walk straight across the next field to a stile by a gate on the far side, then follow the fence on the right to the next stile, then the wall on the left, which curves left to join a track. Pass through the stile by the gate ahead and follow the track up to the houses of West Morton. Pass through the next gate and walk along in front of the houses. Ignore a walled lane coming down from the left and keep straight on. When the tarmac bears right through a gate into a farm, walk straight ahead over the grass to a stile. Now follow the wall on your right through three fields, then walk forward through the trees to join a track and turn right down it.

The track bears left through a wooden gate into Dene Hole Farm, but our way goes through the stile by the large gate to the right of it, through the yard and another large metal gate and on down the field with the wall to the left. Bear left into a walled lane, but where this turns right again go through the stile ahead and walk along the right hand edge of the field to the next stile, which leads into another short section of walled lane. At its end pass through the stile and keep forward along the track with an old wall to your right. Pass to the right of the wall end ahead onto a track which now has a wall on the left. Where the wall ends go through the gateway and walk down the track, now with a wall again on your right, to a gate out onto a road.

Turn right along the road, which curves right, and just after a double gate on the left go through the stile on the left leading into an enclosed footpath. When you reach the houses at East Morton, the path bears right. At a junction of tracks keep straight forward down the left hand track, but after 50 yards fork left down another track which leads to the main street in East Morton. Turn left, pass Green End Road and a few yards after the telephone kiosk turn right down Little Lane, a cobbled road. Walk forward through the yard and through a gate into an enclosed path. This leads to another cobbled yard: walk forward down the access road and turn left at the T-junction (a sign says Cliffe Mill Fold) down the hill, but after 20 yards turn right down an enclosed path. Morton Beck is to your left, and you soon cross it by Hebble Bridge.

Continue up the walled lane. The track becomes surfaced at the houses of Peas Acre, bends left and then right up to the road in Micklethwaite. Turn left uphill. There are benches by the green. As the road bends left round the green, go through the small gate by a large one on the right (by The Bungalow) and follow the track across the field to the next stile by a gate. Pass to the left of the buildings of Fairlady Farm and leave the field by a stile by a gate. Follow the wall/fence on your right. After the next gate the path becomes enclosed, and you follow it to the next road. Cross this and turn left steeply uphill. At the road junction at the top of the hill keep forward for a few yards, then take the signposted path on the right, through a small gate, down some steps and down through the wood.

The path becomes enclosed and leads down to a junction of streets. Keep straight forward down Pinedale opposite to find the continuation of the enclosed path. On the way down you cross the access drive to Gawthorpe Hall, built c.1595, the seat in the Middle Ages of the Lords of the Manor, along to the right. Follow the path down to another access road, walk down this and then turn right along the next road. At the next junction turn left down Beck Lane, which leads back to the canal at the Five Rise Locks.

Bingley Five Rise Locks were built in 1774 and are one of the highlights of the canal. Turn left along the towpath. Swing bridge 201 is at the Three-Rise Locks, and if you are aiming to catch the waterbus to Shipley cross the canal here and follow the new path down to the terminus. To return to Bingley Station do not cross the canal. Having passed under the road bridge and come to the end of the new high wall on the right, go through a gap in the old wall a few yards further on and cross the car park to its exit. Walk up towards Safeway's, but take the first street on the right, Waterloo Road, then the first left, Wellington Street, which leads back to the station.

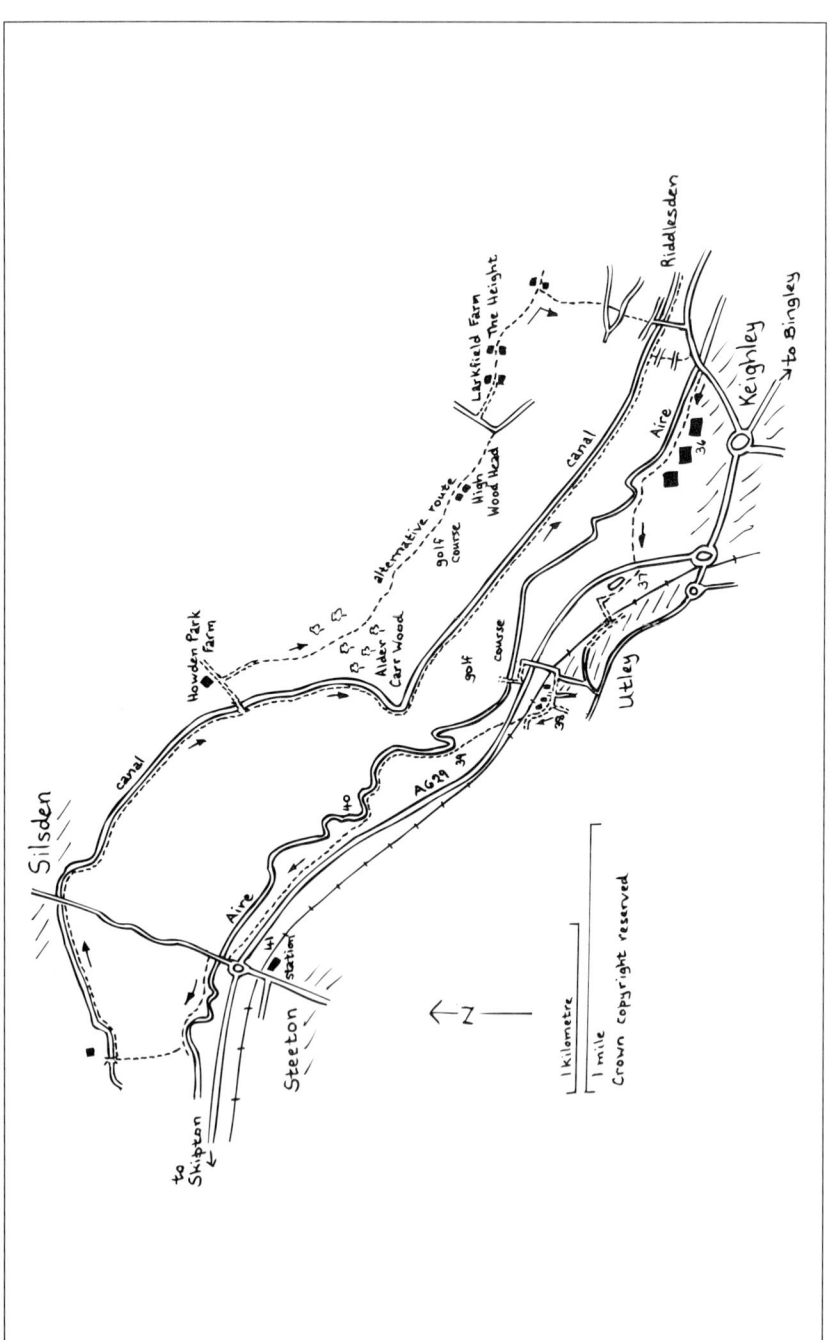

2.3   Keighley to Steeton

South Pennines Outdoor Leisure Map. I suggest that you start and finish at Steeton Station, walking the return half of the walk by the canal first, then returning to Steeton along the Way. Cars may be parked on Aireworth Road, Keighley, which you walked down on the previous walk. Refreshments are available at The Bridge Inn, Riddlesden and The Roebuck, Utley, and on the return route at The Bridge, Silsden and on the higher level alternative at The Willow Tree, Riddlesden.

From the station platforms go up the steep steps to the main road and turn right away from Steeton village. Go clockwise round the roundabout across the main A629 Skipton-Keighley road and head forward in the direction of Addingham on the A6034. Cross the bridge over the Aire and a short distance further on follow the footpath sign on the left down some steps into a very large field. Bear left to the river, then right along the flood bank. (The right of way actually crosses the field, but it's more pleasant to follow the flood bank.) The flood bank makes a long sweep to the right and you reach a stile in a facing fence beside a gate. Cross this and continue along the river bank, crossing another stile (with a gate to the right) and continue along the left hand edge of the field. Towards the end of this field the track bears to the left, but you keep straight on towards a white post in the hedge.

Do not cross the beck and the stile by the white post, but turn right along a clear path with the beck to your left. Cross the stile in the wall ahead (there is another white post) and continue forward to the next stile by a gate. Follow the edge of the next field up to a gap-stile to the right of a gate, which gives access to the canal towpath. Turn right along it. The whole of the next section of the canal is higher than Airedale and gives pleasant views across it.

Having passed under bridge 191A, the Bridge Inn is on your right and by climbing the steps and turning right over the bridge you could make a diversion into Silsden. When you reach Holden Bridge, swing bridge 193, you have a choice of route. If you would prefer a higher route than the towpath, with much better views over Airedale, jump to [#] below. Otherwise continue by the canal. Spring Crag and Alder Carr Woods are now ahead on the other side of the canal, and for a short distance the latter abuts on the canal. The stretch from bridge 194 to Keighley is particularly attractive, including banks of rhododendrons and woodland on the left and a golf course on the right. After bridge 196 you reach Keighley. Look out for the ginnel down to the right, which starts where the row of houses close to the canal on the right ends, and jump to [+] below.

[#] For the high level alternative, leave the towpath by turning left over the bridge and walk up the walled lane to Holden Bridge Farm. Enter the yard, but leave it again by a gate on the right which leads into another walled lane. Follow this to its end, go through the right hand of the two gates and continue along the track with a wall to your left. Pass through the next gate (there is an old step-stile beside it) and follow the track to pass through another gate, a few metres to the left of a pylon. Bear left up the next field, following the power lines but keeping to the left of them, to a stile into Alder Carr Wood. Follow the same line up through the wood on a broad path, quite a stiff climb, still parallel to the power lines. When the gradient eases, the path leads under the power lines, then continues climbing to leave the wood by a stile beside a walled up gateway.

Keep on the same line up the grassy track, passing to the right of a section of old wall, cross the ladder-stile by the gate at the top, then cross the next field to the gateway just to the right of the pylon, but instead of going through, bear right along the top edge of the field with the wall to your left. Now enjoy the views! Cross the ladder-stile and walk along the top edge of the golf course, crossing a broken wall on the way. At the far end of the golf course cross the stile and Clough Beck and keep forward to the wall corner, then keep the wall to your right to a gate. Through this, continue forward to join the access road to the houses of High Wood Head and follow this to the next road. Turn left uphill, then right along the next farm access drive, to Larkfield Farm.

Follow the road straight through the farm, along the cobbles beside the old farmhouse, pass through a small metal gate and cross the next field towards the left hand end of the buildings of The Height Farm. Go through the gate at the farm, then left for a few metres to join a concrete track on which you turn right through the farmyard. In front of the farmhouse turn left, go through the gate out of the farmyard and follow the track to the next farm. Bear slightly left into the yard, then immediately right, down the right hand side of the buildings with a beck on your right. Follow the track and beck down to the houses, go through a large gate and on down the track to pass between the houses to reach a road. Cross this and turn right, but opposite The Willow Tree pub turn left down a cobbled ginnel. Cross straight over the next road and continue down the ginnel. Cross the next road and turn left, then take the next road on the right, cross the canal by the bridge and turn right along the towpath. When you reach the high wooden fence of a bungalow garden, turn left down the footpath. Now you have rejoined the main route.

[+] Walk down the ginnel, crossing the ends of two streets and straight over a third, down the track opposite (the left hand track), which curves slightly left. Pass through the yard between sheds and climb the steps to the road. Turn right over the Aire bridge. Immediately beyond it turn right again at the footpath signpost down some more steps. You are now back on the Airedale Way.

Follow the riverside path, soon passing the car park of the Bridge pub, and then for some distance you have factories on your

left, at first bounded by a high wall, then a fence. Follow this fence along, at one point leaving the riverside briefly, then when the fence makes a sharp turn left, go with it, and now you are back by the river. When the fence makes another sharp turn left, pass through the stile and follow the riverbank to the start of a hedge. Keep to the left of the hedge and you will soon find yourself in the remains of an old hedged footpath, which soon bears right and then left again. Follow this path to its end - if it is too overgrown, divert to the adjacent field - and when the hedge finally peters out you will see a stile in the fence ahead, with a public footpath sign beyond, and a path slanting up right from it. So cross the track by the two stiles and make your way up to the dual carriageway.

Breaks in the crash barriers enable you to cross this busy road, then drop left to the next stile and footpath sign. Cross the stile and bear right along the track, in a few yards keeping right at a fork, then bearing left in front of the pond, an old meander of the Aire. Follow the track along to a cross track and turn left. Cross the railway by the footbridge - ahead is the start of the very large Utley Cemetery - and turn right along the walled lane. Pass under a bridge linking two parts of the cemetery to reach the village of Low Utley, a charming spot with some lovely old houses. Keep forward along the road, bearing left with it at the fork, then ignore Birchwood Drive on the left and turn right down the cobbled Keelham Lane *(by following the road up you would soon reach the Roebuck).*

On reaching a T-junction with a stone wall ahead, the right hand branch, the access road to Keighley Golf Course, crosses a railway bridge, but we turn left along a walled lane. Cross straight over the access road to a new residential development and keep on along the old walled lane until on a left hand bend you reach the railway. Cross the stile, then the railway (taking care, because this is a busy line), then the stile on the far side, then follow the wall on your right to the next stile. Cross the dual carriageway once again, then the next very high ladder-stile, and keep following the wall on your right until near a wall corner there is a gateway straight ahead with a gap stile just to the right of it and another old stone gatepost a few yards to the left.

Cross the stile and head over the next field towards a power line pole, then maintain the same line towards a white notice by the river (Keighley Angling Club: Private Fishing) and keep forward along the river bank. At the end of the Keighley Angling Club stretch you are faced by a fence: cross this and keep on by the river until you come quite close to the boundary fence of the dual carriageway and reach a wall on the right. Cross the step-stile and walk straight across the next field to a gap-stile by a gateway in the wall on the far side.

Now bear slightly left, keeping below the river flood bank, and walk across the large field to a stile in the fence on the left, and from it bear very slightly left to a gap-stile in the next facing wall. Now go half left to the stile already visible in the next wall, then straight over the next field, parallel to the road to your left, crossing a deep drainage ditch near the fence on the left. Cross the step-stile about 15 yards to the right of the next wall corner and walk straight over the next field to pass to the right of a wooden shed and up a track to a stile and the road. The Airedale Way continues by crossing the road and turning right over the river bridge.

To return to Steeton Station cross the road and turn left to the roundabout, go round this anti-clockwise, then straight on.

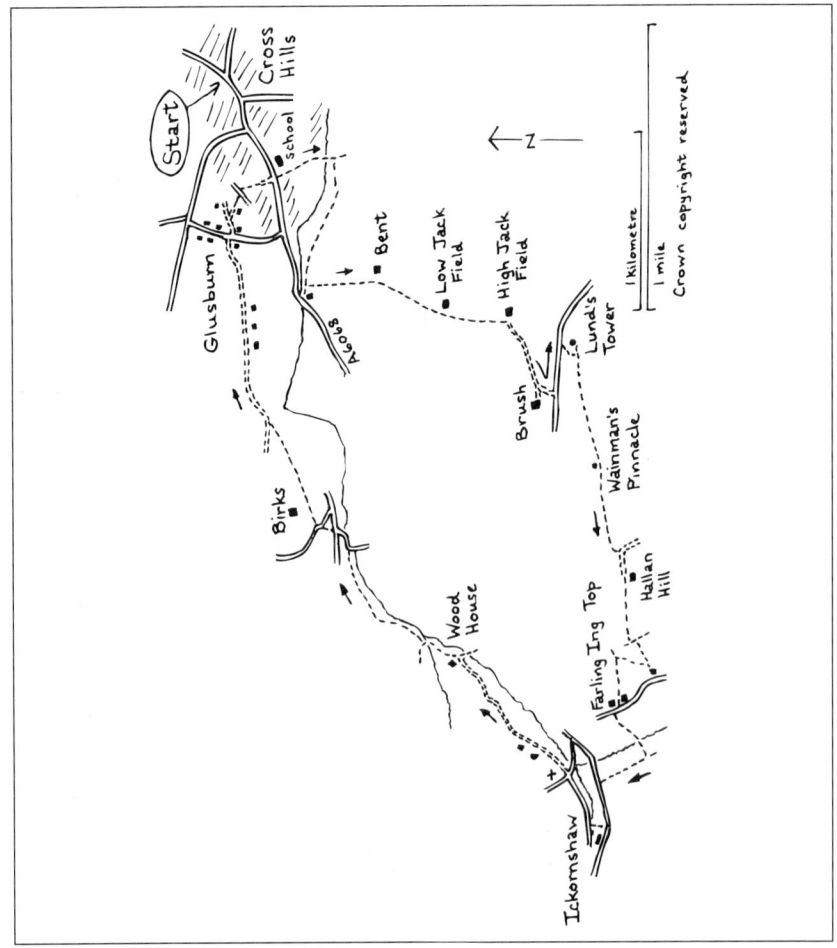

Correction

page 32, line 6, <u>delete</u>:
Cross the step-stile ... straight over the next field
and <u>substitute</u>:
Where the fence becomes a hedge, cross the stile in it and bear right to follow the fence on your left until you reach a cross wall. Turn right along it, ignoring a gap in it, and go through the gap ahead, then turn left through the next field

A Walk to the Cowling Pinnacles and Ickornshaw.

South Pennines Outdoor Leisure Map. Start and finish in Cross Hills. 7¾ miles (12.4 km). Superb views and quiet, pastoral countryside. A moderate grade walk, as there are some steepish slopes, and one rather deep beck to be crossed, which can be fun!

By bus: Keighley & District 66/66A (Keighley-Skipton), 68A/22/24/25/25A (Keighley-Burnley) to Main Street, Cross Hills.

By car: There is a free car park, signposted from the main road, behind the Coop Food Fayre in Cross Hills. There are toilets nearby on the other side of the main road.

Walk along Cross Hills Main Street in the direction of Glusburn, pass Glusburn County Primary School and immediately turn left past a bollard along a tarmac lane. At the end of the playing fields follow the lane past houses, cross Holme Beck by a footbridge and immediately fork right along a path with a wood to the right and a fence to the left. At the end of the fenced path cross a stile into a field and follow the clear path as it bears slightly left to a gateway in the next wall. Walk across the next field towards a fence and trees, cross a stile in the fence and follow the enclosed path to where it ends at another stile. By walking straight on you would reach the main road at Glusburn Bridge, but instead turn left up another enclosed path to a stile and farm access road.

Follow the road up, but 10 yards after crossing a cattle grid cross the stile in the fence on the right and continue up the left hand edge of the field to a stile by a gate in the top corner at Bent Farm. Go left for three yards then turn right up the tarmac road. Keep up the track, Jackfield Lane, to Low Jackfield Farm, where it ends. Cross the stile by the gate ahead and follow the hedge/wall to your right up to High Jackfield Farm, then bear right up the farm access road to the next motor road. Now the views begin to open up. Turn left up the road, but where it begins to curve slightly right, take the track slanting right through the heather. It leads through an old quarry, then turn left up to the top of the escarpment. Turn left for Lund's Tower, which can be climbed. The views are magnificent.

Now walk along the edge of the escarpment to Wainman's Pinnacle. *The Wainmans were once important landowners in the neighbourhood, but no one really knows why this obelisk was erected: is it a memorial to someone who was killed in the Civil War or the Napoleonic Wars? does it celebrate the successful end of these latter? is it simply to add something to the view from the local big house, Carr Head?* From the Pinnacle keep on down the ridge, but when you draw level with a wall corner over on the left, bear left and pass through the second of two gates, then follow the track to Hallan Hill Farm. Walk straight through the yard, passing to the right of all the buildings, and through a gate into a field. Follow the wall on your left to the next stile, just to the right of a gate facing you, then keep on in the same direction until you drop more steeply to the bottom corner of a field. Cross the stile on the left and walk forward to pass the head of a beck, then immediately cross the stile on the right and follow the right hand edge of the field towards the next farm, soon with a wall to your right.

About 30 yards before the farm cross a stile in this wall and walk down for a few yards with a wall on your left, before bearing half right over the field to pass through a gate in a fence just to the right of the end of a wall near the bottom right hand corner. Walk forward for a yard or two to meet a cross path and turn left up it. Walk straight across the middle of the field to a wall corner opposite, pass through the stile and continue with the wall to your left. On approaching the houses at Farling Ing Top go through the small gate beside the large gate and follow the track forward to a road. Cross and go through the kissing gate opposite. Walk down the field with a fence to your right, and just after a gate in it cross a step stile in the wall and turn left down the left hand edge of the next field. When the wall turns left, keep straight forward, cross an old stile in a broken down cross wall, then walk steeply down to a stile in the fence at the bottom. This is a lovely spot. Across the beck there is another stile, but the beck between flows fast and deep: it is however shallower and can be forded more easily further to the left. Climb steeply up the far side through the trees with a fence to your right and when the gradient eases cross to the wall on the right and follow it up until you reach a gate in it. Go through and head over the next field towards a wall corner beyond a solitary tree. Keeping the wall on your left, follow it along until you emerge onto the A6068.

Cross the road and turn left. The Pennine Way joins us over a stile on the left, and we follow it for about 300 yards! The Black Bull (open all day, every day) is a short distance further along, at the furthest point of our walk, but our route turns right before it, shortly after a bus shelter, following the Pennine Way sign, down a well trodden path into Ickornshaw. Turn right along the road. Soon the Pennine Way turns left up a cobbled track (there are toilets at the top) but we follow the road to the next junction and cross straight over Gill Lane to pass through a stile beside a large gate, with Cowling Parish Church to the left and the Old Vicarage to the right. Follow the track until you reach a large shed on the right of it, then pass through the stile to the right of the right hand of the two large gates ahead and continue along the track with a wall to your left.

The track descends to pass Wood House Farm, and at a fork, with a paved path coming up from the right, bear left. The track narrows to a path and crosses Gill Beck by a footbridge. Turn right and follow a wall on the right along to pass through a small gate beside a large one into the pleasant parkland of Carr Head Hall. Keep along parallel to the beck. Just after passing a gate, note an old limekiln to the left. At one point there is even a bench! Follow the beck until you are able to cross it by a footbridge. Turn left along the road over Lane Ends Bridge. At the T-junction cross to the stile a yard to the left, walk down the steps and the field and emerge onto the next road. Walk forward over Birks Bridge and just beyond the second gate go through a stile on the right and walk across the field to the next stile to the left of another gate.

Now walk straight over the next field parallel to the beck with Birks Farm up to the left to a gap in the hedge on the far side. Continue forward to the next stile, leaving the beck, cross the footbridge and walk up the steep slope opposite. Follow the hedge on the left to a stile in the corner of the field, then on to the gate in the next field corner, and now the hedge is on your right. The next gate gives access to a farm road, which is followed all the way to the next motor road. Here turn right, but after the first house on the left turn left along Ryecroft Road, an unsurfaced track. At a fork keep right through a metal gate, and at the next street cross diagonally left to go down the ginnel opposite. At the end bear left down the track to reach the main road. Turn left to return to Cross Hills.

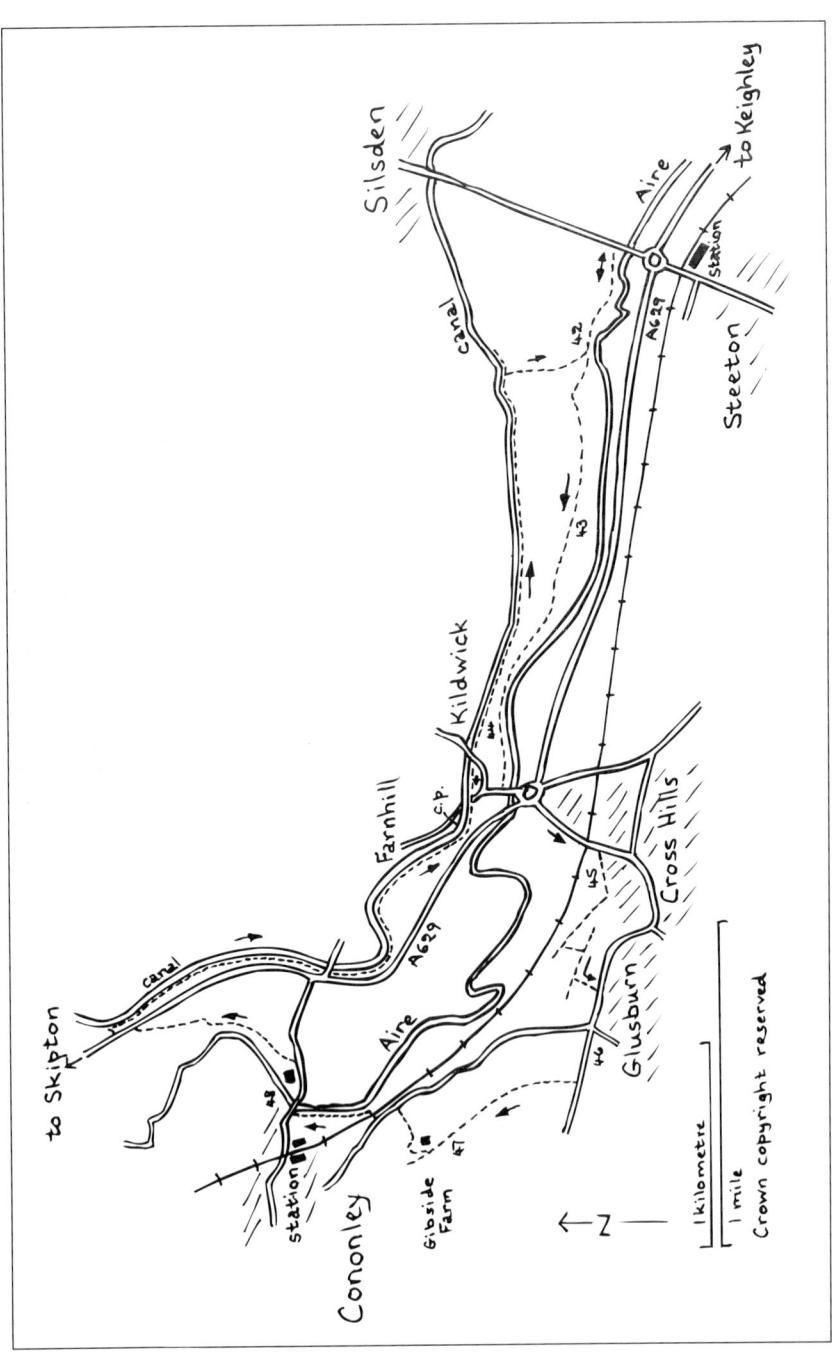

Stage 3 Steeton to Gargrave (12¼ miles, 19.8 km)

This stage can be divided into three shorter walks:
3.1 Steeton to Cononley (9 miles, 14.6 km)
3.2 Cononley to Skipton (8¼ miles, 13.3 km)
3.3 Skipton to Gargrave (9½ miles, 15.3 km)

3.1 Steeton Station to Cononley

South Pennines Outdoor Leisure Map. Start and finish at Steeton Station. There is a small car park by Cononley station, or park in the village. Cononley was once a major estate of Bolton Abbey, later busy with workers in the Duke of Devonshire's nearby lead mines. The attractive village contains a number of fine old houses. Refreshments are available at The White Lion, Kildwick and at pubs in Cononley. On the A629 just north of Farnhill Bridge there is a large layby, where there is usually a trailer with refreshments, with paths up onto the canal towpath. By the canal in Farnhill there are a car park and public telephone, with a small children's playground and picnic site.

From the station platforms go up the steep steps to the main road and turn right away from Steeton village. Go clockwise round the roundabout across the main A629 Skipton-Keighley road and head forward in the direction of Addingham on the A6034. Cross the bridge over the Aire and a short distance further on follow the footpath sign on the left down some steps into a very large field.

Bear left to the river, then right along the flood bank. (The right of way actually crosses the field, but it's more pleasant to follow the flood bank.) The flood bank makes a long sweep to the right and you reach a stile in a facing fence beside a gate. Cross this and continue along the river bank, crossing another stile (with a gate to the right) and continue along the left hand edge of the field. Towards the end of this field the track bears to the left, but you keep straight on towards a white post in the hedge. Having crossed the beck and the stile by the white post, walk slightly right over the field to the white post opposite and bear right along by the hedge. The white posts make navigation easy on the next stretch. Walk along the left hand edge of the field, which curves left, and when you reach a cross track coming across the field from the right, turn left, cross a ditch and turn right along the left hand edge of the next field with a hedge to your left, and when the hedge/fence on the left makes a right-angle bend to the right and becomes a wall follow it, then when the wall turns left go left with it and follow it to a stile to the right of a gate in the corner of the field.

Bear slightly right and follow the white posts across the next field to the fence/hedge opposite. *On the left is another old river meander. Flooding used to be common in the Aire valley, but by the*

Airedale Drainage Act of 1861 the river bed between Skipton and Bingley was deepened and straightened. **Cross the stile and keep your line over the next field to the next white post and stile.** *There's another old meander to your left.* **The stile is a few yards to the right of the point where the wall joins the fence. Cross the low embankment ahead and continue by the fence/hedge on your left. In the corner of this field there is a path junction: ignore the path turning right and following the wall up to a gate, and keep straight ahead over the stile and on by the fence/hedge to your left.**

At the far end of the field there is a stile in the fence on the left by a gate, with some sheep pens ahead. Cross the stile and turn right along the track to the next stile by another gate. Now you are back by the Aire. Follow the floodbank all the way to Kildwick Bridge, *the oldest bridge over the Aire, built by the monks of Bolton Abbey in 1305; in 1780 the bridge was widened, and the four eastern arches (which one sees from this side) were all made round; on the other side there are two pointed and two round arches, which are older. The logo of the Airedale Way is based on this bridge.* **Here a stile gives access to the road.** *A short distance to the right is The White Lion and Kildwick village. St.Andrew's church, dating from the 14th and 15th centuries, is about 165 feet long, which earns it the name of The Long Kirk of Craven. Kildwick church and manor were given by the Romilly family of Skipton Castle to the monks of Bolton Abbey. After the Dissolution the village and manor were purchased by the Currer family, who lived in the 17th century Hall until early this century.* **Cross the road and turn left to cross the river. Immediately after the bridge turn right along a tarmac footpath which leads under the A629. Now you must leave the river again for a time. When the tarmac path ends keep forward along the footway into Glusburn.**

Cross the railway, and after the first houses on the right but before the Esso garage turn right over a stile and follow the ginnel to another stile into a field. Follow the fence on the left, pass through a gap in an old fence, then an iron kissing-gate, and keep forward up the path to join a track. Turn right along it, but only for a few yards, because when the track turns left and there is a private access drive ahead, fork half right down to a metal gate leading into an enclosed paved path. At the end of this cross a stone stile into the next field, and follow the clear path to the next stile opposite, then straight over the next field to the next stile. *Sharp Haw beyond Skipton is now visible.*

Cross the stile and turn sharp left up with the wall on your left. Pass through a kissing-gate out of the field and up a ginnel to a street. Turn right along it. When the street ends and you reach a redundant kissing-gate at the start of a farm access road, turn left

just before this through a gate and up a tarmac path into a public park. *(There are toilets down to the left here. The park would be a nice spot for a picnic.)* **Keep forward uphill, passing to the left of a shelter with benches and to the right of a children's playground, and when you approach the top edge of the park turn left to reach the exit onto a road. Turn right up the footway. Keep straight ahead at the crossroads, along Lothersdale Road.** *The Cowling Pinnacles on Earl Crag are visible over to the left.*

After 300 yards cross the signposted stile on the right and walk along the track with a wall to your right. Go through the kissing-gate at the far end of the field and keep forward along the track, with lovely views over Airedale. Having passed through a stile in the wall on the right, keep forward along the track. Pass through a kissing-gate by a gate and follow the track to the next gate, with Gibside Farm down on the right. Beyond the gate the track forks: go right through the gate and follow the track as it curves down through the field, leaving it by a cattle grid. Turn left down the farm road to the motor road and turn left along this.

About 10 yards before the start of the 30 mph limit cross the stile on the right, then the railway line, then the next stile, to return to the Aire. Follow the riverbank. *This would be a nice spot for a picnic.* **A kissing-gate gives access to an enclosed path. Leave this by a stile and walk forward to the next stile onto the road. The Airedale Way continues by crossing the road to the stile opposite and going down the steps.**

About 200 yards to the left is Cononley Station. To return to Steeton turn right and cross the river. Pass a row of terrace houses and the Yorkshire Dales Old fashioned Dairy Ice-cream factory on the left, then 20 yards before the end of the 30 mph limit cross the stile in a short section of wall on the left, go down the steps and bear slightly right over the field to the riverbank, then right along it. When you are faced by a hedge, ignore the stiles ahead and turn right alongside it, to the gated stile on the left in the field corner. Cross it and bear slightly right over the next field to the stile in the opposite wall. Keep your line across the next field, heading for the arrows indicating a right bend on the road ahead. A stile leads out onto the road. Cross and turn left for a few yards, then right up a track which leads to the canal towpath. Turn right along it.

On this walk too the canal is at a fairly high level, giving pleasant views over Airedale. Unfortunately a stretch is close to the noisy main road. Bridge 183A is Farnhill Bridge. The large house up on the left is Farnhill Hall, which goes back to the early 14th century; the tower-like block facing the canal is early 16th century. By crossing swing bridge 185 a detour through Farnhill is possible. Stone bridge 186 gives access to St.Andrew's Church, Kildwick. Just below the church is The White Lion.

After passing swing bridge 187 look up left for a view of the finest house around here, the 17th-century Kildwick Hall. Leave the towpath at swing bridge 191 by turning right over a stile to the left of a large gate, and walk down the track close to the right hand edge of the field. Cross the stile by the gate ahead and keep down the edge of the next field. Shortly a path leads up onto the banking on the right. At the far end of this field cross the stile in the wall ahead and continue along the top of the bank. When you draw level with a white post on the right, turn sharp left, join the track and follow it back to Steeton by your outward route.

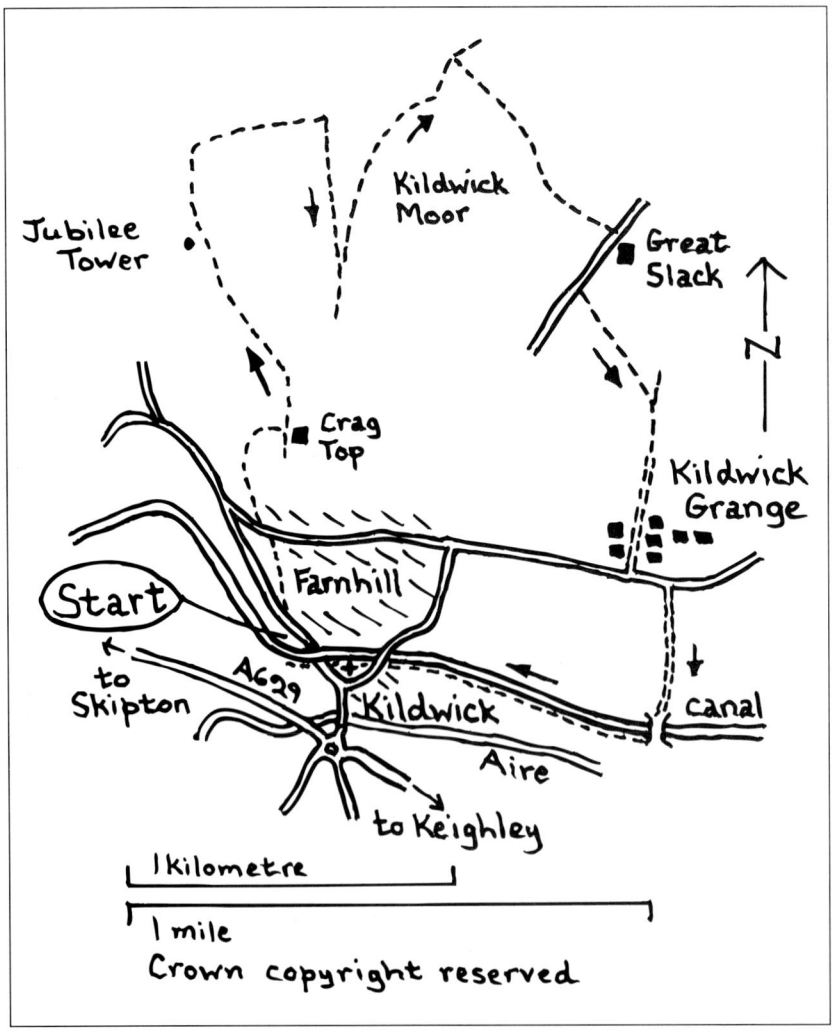

A Walk from Kildwick to the Jubilee Tower
South Pennines Outdoor Leisure Map. 4 miles (6.4 km). A walk up to the Jubilee Tower on Farnhill Moor is hard to resist. It is a superb viewpoint for Airedale, and can be reached in about twenty minutes from the canalside car park. It is of course possible to walk up to it and straight down again, but a pleasant circular walk can be made which takes in the most attractive settlement of Kildwick Grange, once a farm owned by Bolton Abbey. This walk, partly over heather moorland, is at its best in August.

By car: Turn off the A629 and drive through Kildwick, past the church and under the canal, then turn left and there on the right is the car park.

By bus: Keighley and District no. 68 and 78, Keighley to Skipton, Monday to Saturday, will drop you on the old A629 at Kildwick. From the bus stop walk along to the village and turn left up past the church. Just before the road goes under the canal, there's a public footpath on the right up to the towpath. Turn left along it to the next swing bridge and cross this to reach the ginnel at the start of the walk.

There's a very infrequent service, the no.70 Keighley to Skipton via Farnhill and Low Bradley, Monday to Saturday, which will drop you on the top road in Farnhill. From the bus stop walk in the Skipton direction; the road begins to descend, you pass a street called The Arbour on the left and then go through the kissing gate on the right: start the description at [*] below. To return to this bus route at the end of the walk, cross the stone canal bridge by the church and walk straight up to reach the road, turning left to the bus stop.

A few yards beyond the telephone kiosk at the end of the car park take the cobbled ginnel on the right. Ignore a right fork on the way up by a lamppost, and when you reach a double concrete track on a bend, keep straight up along it to the next road. Turn left along it for a few yards, then [*] go through the kissing-gate on the right and up the access drive. About 150 yards along fork right off the drive up a narrower footpath, soon through bracken, then through heather. At one point the clear path drops quite steeply into a little valley, which you walk up and climb out of at the far end and reach a track. Turn right along this, but after a few yards fork left off it again up a footpath.

Turn left in front of the house, Crag Top, cross the step stile and follow the broad track across Farnhill Moor. Ignoring minor paths forking right and left, keep on the main path all the way to the Jubilee Tower, an excellent viewpoint and a fine place for a picnic.

To continue the walk keep on the path which passes the back of the Tower. It is narrow but clear and soon bears slightly right through the heather across the moor. Shortly before the boundary wall the path bears right again and soon you are walking parallel to this wall on your left. When you draw level with a small pond on the other side of the wall, the path bears right yet again, away from the wall, back across the moor. After a while you begin to descend and come close to a wall on the left. When you are about 20 yards from this wall, look out for a narrow path coming in from over your left shoulder. When you locate it, turn sharp left along it, back up the moor parallel to the wall, which of course is now on your right.

Follow this path up nearly to the top of the moor, where you will reach a ladder stile (and an old stone step-stile) in the wall on the right. Cross this onto Kildwick Moor and bear half left on a clear path to another ladder stile in the wall corner. Cross this and walk straight over the next field, bearing slightly away from the wall on your right, to reach a step-stile in the facing wall. Now turn right and follow the wall on your right. Cross a step-stile, pass the top side of a small wood, cross a gap-stile near the far end of the wood (the wall has collapsed a few yards to the left of this stile) and when a short distance further on the wall turns right to a corner, cut this corner and walk to the gap-stile opposite.

Aim now for the right hand end of the wood ahead, cross the ladder stile and walk down the side of the wood with the wall to your left. At the end of the wood bear left and keep following the wall on your left to the next very tall ladder stile. Keep forward to the stile in the fence ahead and turn right along the road. Pass Great Slack Farm, and just before you reach the next (ruined) farm on the left (Little Slack) cross the stile on the left, walk down a very short section of walled lane and bear slightly right across the field to a stile in the wall on the far side. Bear half left over the next field to the next stile in a short section of wall, then keep the same line over the next field to a stile in the far corner. Turn right and follow the wall on your right to the stile in the next corner. Go left across the next field to a stile onto a walled lane and turn right down this.

It leads to a gate and the road down through the very attractive and nicely restored old houses of Kildwick Grange. At the next road turn left, but opposite the next group of houses on the left turn down the walled lane on the right. Follow this track down to the canal, cross the swing bridge and turn right along the towpath to return to the start of the walk.

A Circular Walk from Cononley to Lothersdale

South Pennines Outdoor Leisure Map. 9 miles (14.3 km). Start and finish at Cononley Station. Car parking at the station or in the village. Peaceful pastoral countryside, old farmhouses, heather moorland and superb views.

From the station walk up the main road through the village. Immediately before The Institute (with the clock tower) turn left along a track, passing Shackleton Ghyll Farm. Go through the gate by the cattle-grid and up the access road to Town Head Farm. Where the road turns right to the farm, keep forward up the walled lane to a gate at the top (look back for the fine view over Airedale), then continue along the track with the wall to your right. At the far end of the field cross the stile between the two gates and continue with the wall to your right until you reach Great Gib Farm. Pass to the left of the farm and keep on to pass to the left of the next house, Little Gib. Immediately at the end of the house cross a stile on the left and bear slightly right up the field to cross a ladder-stile in the top corner.

Bear half left across the next field, passing to the right of the old lead mine once developed by the Duke of Devonshire, soon on a track which passes through a gateway then follows a wall on the right. When you reach Manor House Farm, enter the yard and bear left along the back of the buildings, then at the end of the farmhouse turn right and walk straight down the access road to the Lothersdale Road, where you turn right. Turn left down the next farm access road to Well House, cross the cattle-grid and keep left at the fork, with a wall to your left. Follow this down, passing through two gates, then at the bottom of the next field follow the track through the right hand of the two gates and on down to Cook House Farm.

When you reach it, don't go through the gate into the yard but turn right along the bottom of the field to pass to the back of the farm and reach a step-stile in the field corner. Now follow the wall on your left to the next road. Turn right but towards the end of Leys Laithe Farm opposite cross the stile on the left, turn sharp right between a wooden shed and the wall to the next stile, then bear half left over the field to a wall corner. Follow this wall on your right, with the valley of Leys Beck down to your left, to Leys House. Cross the step-stile and walk straight forward between the houses, across the yard, through two old stone gateposts and over the grass to a stile in the next facing wall, then slightly right to the next stile.

Follow the wall/fence on your right along, cross the ladder-stile in the field corner and bear left along the wall on your left to the next stile, then continue along the top side of the wood to the far end. Cross the

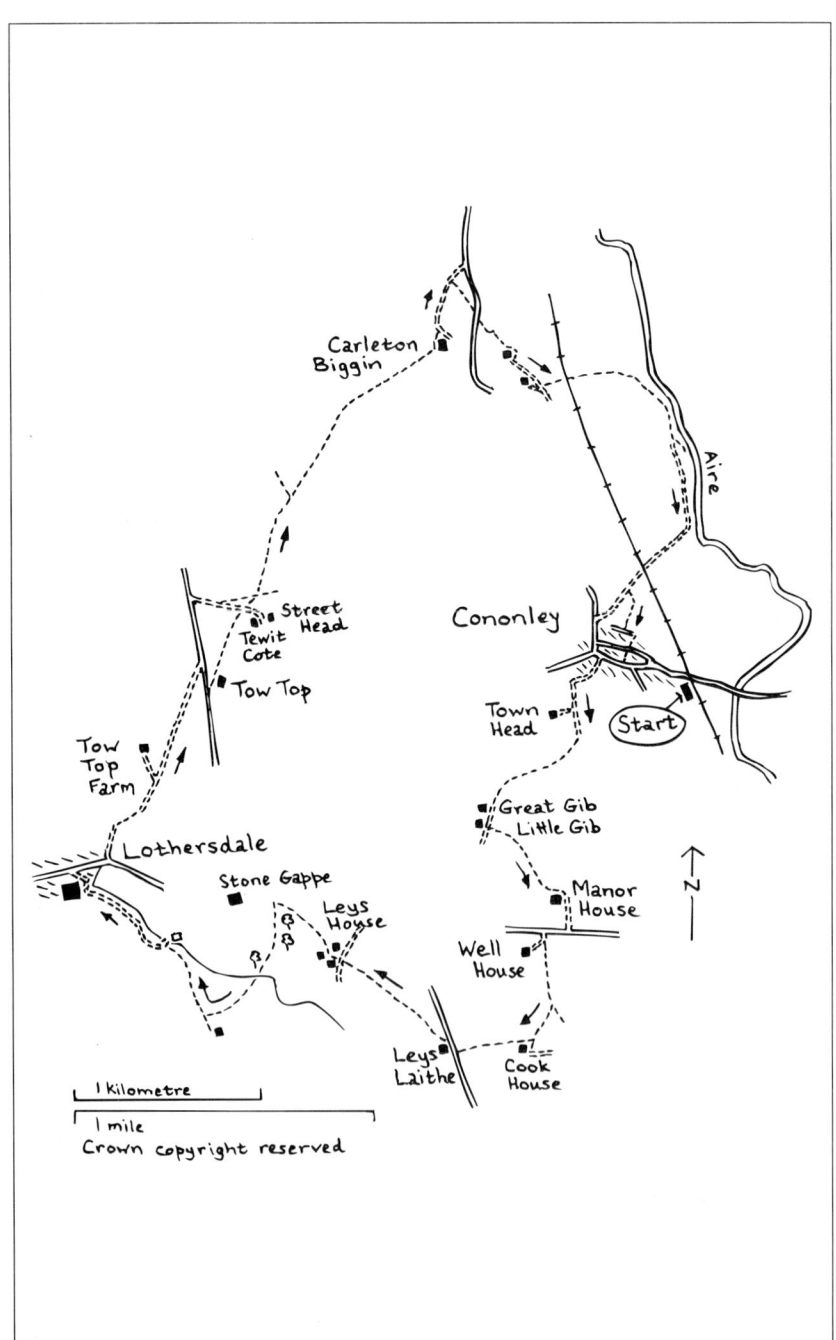

stile on the left and walk down the edge of the wood with a wall to your right. The wall ends at a stile by an old gateway: keep straight on down. *The large house up to the right is Stone Gappe, dating from Norman times and the ancient seat of the Lace family (note how many names around here on the map have Leys in them); Charlotte Brontë was governess here for a short time, and Gateshead Hall in Jane Eyre was modelled on this house.*

Pass another old field boundary and keep on down, but after about 50 yards bear slightly right down the field on a faint path, keep to the left of some trees at a spring and follow them down to a footbridge over the beck.

Bear half right over the next field to a wall corner, from which you will see a stile a few yards ahead. Cross this and bear slightly right over the next field to the next stile. Head slightly right up the next field towards the right hand end of the high hedge, where you will find a stile in the fence. Walk forward to cross the next stile in the wall ahead and turn right down the clear path to a stile by a gate into the next field. Now follow the wall on your left along and then down the slope, to cross a stile in the wall at the bottom. Walk forward to cross a little footbridge, then keep forward on level ground towards the sewage works. But they are on the other side of Lothersdale Beck. Pass them and join a track coming over the ford and keep forward along the track with the beck to your right to Lothersdale. There are two benches on this attractive section. When you reach the mill, *originally a water-powered corn mill and later used for cotton spinning and silk weaving,* the track bears right then left round it, and reaches the main road opposite the Hare and Hounds.

Turn right along the road. In a few yards the Pennine Way forks left through a farmyard, but we stay on the road as it begins to climb and crosses Stansfield Beck by a bridge. Immediately fork left off it through a gate up a track signposted to Tow Top Moor. When the enclosed section ends, keep forward on a clear path up the field to re-enter a broad walled lane at the top. The view back is attractive. Through a gate you join the access road to Tow Top Farm. Keep forward up it and follow it to the next motor road. Turn right along the road, then left into the next farm entrance (Tow Top), but go through the stile to the left of the gate and into a field. Follow the wall on your right past the farm, through a gate and over a stile, to where it ends at a stile into a rough pasture, with Tewit Cote and Street Head Farms to the right.

Cross the access track and bear slightly right to the stile in the far corner, crossing another track on the way, which leads through a gate on the right. Cross the stile and follow the wall on your right (sharing for a short distance the route of the Carleton Glen walk). The next stile is to the right of a large gap in the wall, and now the wall is on your left. Follow it down into a dip, cross the stile in it, then turn right and continue with the wall to your right. Follow this wall up to the rise, then down the other side, with superb views over Airedale. A stile leads out of the heather moorland into a field. Keep on by the wall to Carleton Biggin Farm. Cross the stile in the bottom corner, then keep on by the wall to a small gate in the next bottom corner, then bear left down the farm access road.

About 100 yards before the next motor road there is a step-stile in the wall on the left. Turn **right** here and head straight across the grass: out of sight over the brow of the hill there is a step-stile out onto the road. Turn right for 20 yards, cross the gated stile on the left (mind you don't trip on the wire!), and turn half right to contour round the head of a dry valley to a gate in the wall corner opposite. Follow the wall on your right, and where it ends keep forward to pick up a broken wall on the left, which leads to a gate. Go through and keep on with the wall to your right - Throstle Nest is the house - and when the wall turns right keep with it, go through a gate and bear left along the track. Follow this past the next house, and when you reach a junction with the track coming from the house, turn left over the grass with a small beck to your left to a stile in the fence ahead.

Walk down the left hand edge of the next field with the ditch to your left to a stile in the far corner (you will need to jump the ditch to reach it), then cross the railway with great care and the stile on the far side, then follow the fence on your right and the embankment to the next stile, then keep forward along the top of the embankment to the river. Turn right along the bank, joining for a short distance the Airedale Way. When you come to a track, keep forward along it, and stay on it, soon leaving the river bank and the Way. The track becomes a hedged/fenced lane, which leads back to Cononley.

About 100 yards after crossing the railway (again, take great care!) cross a stile by a gateway on the left at a junction of tracks and turn right to follow the wall on your right. Cross the next stile and walk forward for 10 yards, ignoring a clear path on the right, to a gated stile on the right. Walk up the middle of the field to the stile by the gate at the far end, then forward to the street and turn left. Take the ginnel on the right of the parking area at the end, and where it ends either turn left to return to the station or cross the street and walk forward along New Inn Fold to reach the main road by the New Inn.

3.2 Cononley to Skipton

Start and finish at Cononley Station. There is a small car park at the station, or about 200 yards further into the village there is another small car park in Moorfoot Lane, just beyond the Christian Centre. Between it and the station there are a children's playground and toilets. By the canal at Low Bradley there are a car park and a small park with benches, a lovely spot for a picnic. Refreshments can be had at pubs in Cononley and pubs and cafés in Skipton. On the return route there are three pubs by the canal at Snaygill, The King Henry VIII, Randells Hotel and The Bay Horse.

Skipton Castle, built by the Normans to protect the Aire Gap through the Pennines, was held first by the Romillys and then, from 1311, by the Cliffords. The present castle dates largely from the 14th, 16th and 17th centuries and is worth visiting. Holy Trinity Church next door is late mediaeval. The town was granted a market by King John in 1204.

On leaving the station turn right away from the village past a large factory. Immediately before the bridge over the river go through the stile on the left and down a few steps. **For the next four kilometres you follow the riverbank, one of the most peaceful, pastoral sections of the Way. Eventually you pass under the railway line, still by the riverside. Cross the stile in the next fence. Now the right of way leaves the river and crosses the very large field, but there is no clear path and I am sure that it is in everyone's interests if you stay by the river all the way round to Carleton Bridge.** *There is a lot of evidence of usage along the floodbank. Just before the bridge Eller Beck, which flows through Skipton, joins the Aire.* **A stile by the gate on the left of the bridge leads out onto the road. Turn right.** *From here there is no right of way by the river, and instead of several kilometres of road walking via Carleton and Heslaker Lane, which would be the route closest to the river, we shall skirt round Skipton.*

Cross the Aire by Carleton Bridge and follow the road into Skipton, passing under the A629. Pass the crematorium and cemetery and bear right with the road to cross Eller Beck. The road is joined by Burnside Crescent from the right. Turn left at the next junction down Carleton New Road. You cross Eller Beck once more, pass playing fields and then cross the railway, with Skipton Station to the right. The road turns sharp right and drops to turn right again to a T-junction, but at this point you turn left up a narrower road to the canal. Don't cross the swing bridge. The Airedale Way turns left along the towpath.

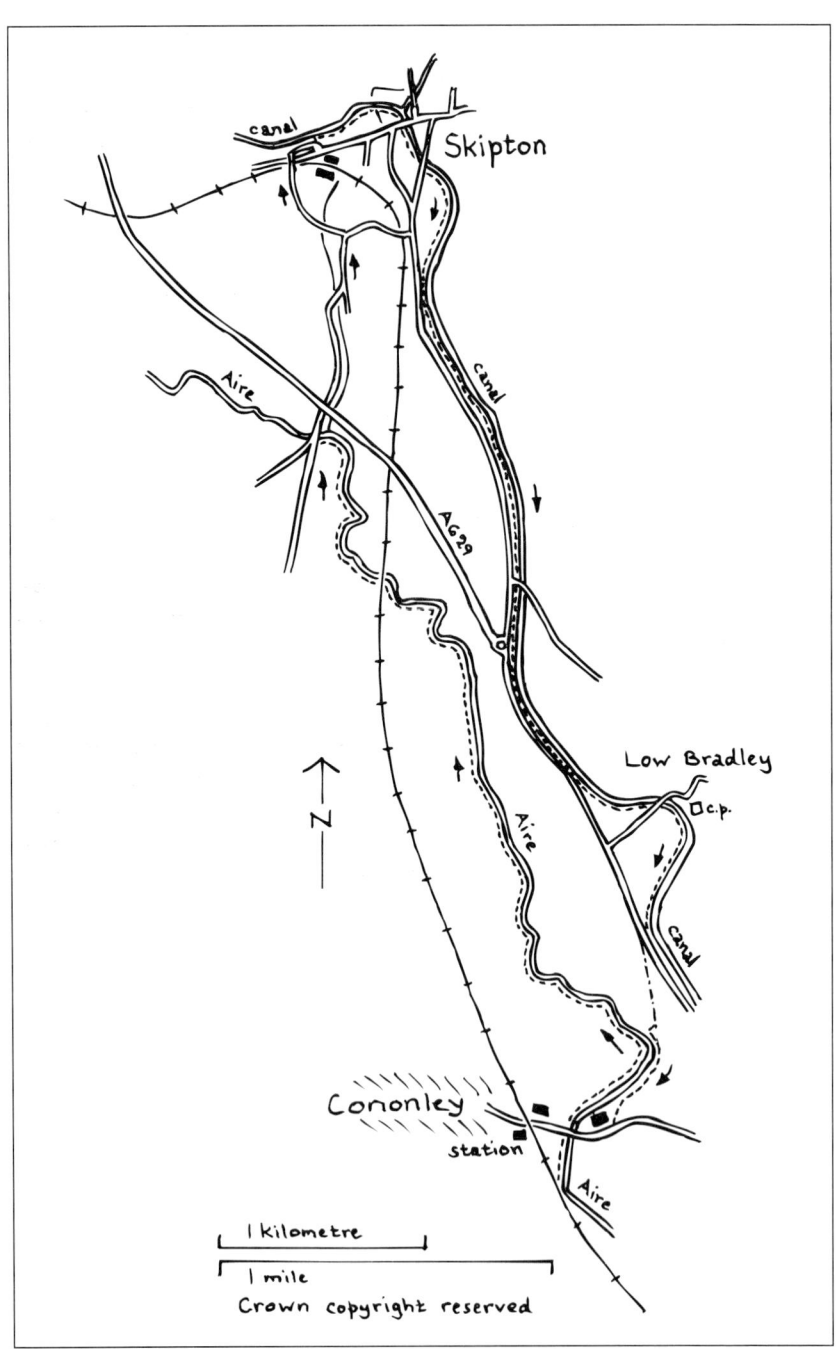

To return to Cononley turn right along the towpath. The towpath is a quiet route through Skipton, but apart from the attraction of the narrow boats moored in the centre it is a pretty dull one. Shortly after swing bridge 177 and before the tall chimney, the canal crosses Eller Beck. By the Boat Shop across the canal there is a canal junction, with the Springs Branch forking left. For the town centre leave the towpath at bridge 178 and cross the bridge.

Having passed under an old stone bridge and reached countryside again, you come to the King Henry VIII pub, and a short distance further on is the large modern Randells Hotel. Immediately after it is swing bridge 181 at Low Snaygill.

After another 300 yards you reach the Bay Horse, which is immediately followed by bridge 182, Snaygill Stone Bridge. Having had the main road just below it for a stretch, the canal curves away from it again and the village of Low Bradley comes into view. Access to it is over swing bridge 182A, and by the bridge there is a small park with benches, a lovely spot for a breather. Leave the canal at swing bridge 183, which is where you joined it on the previous walk, and walk down the track to the main road. Cross this with great care - the corner to the left is blind - and turn left for a few yards to the stile in the wall on the right.

Go down the steps and turn fairly sharp left across the field to a gap-stile visible in the next wall. Cross it and bear slightly right over the next field to the gate in the wall opposite. Cross the stile by the gate and turn right with the hedge to your right to the river. Turn left along the bank. When you are about 100 yards from the ice cream factory a faint path bears half left away from the river across the field to steps up to a stile onto the road. Cross the road and turn right to return to Cononley.

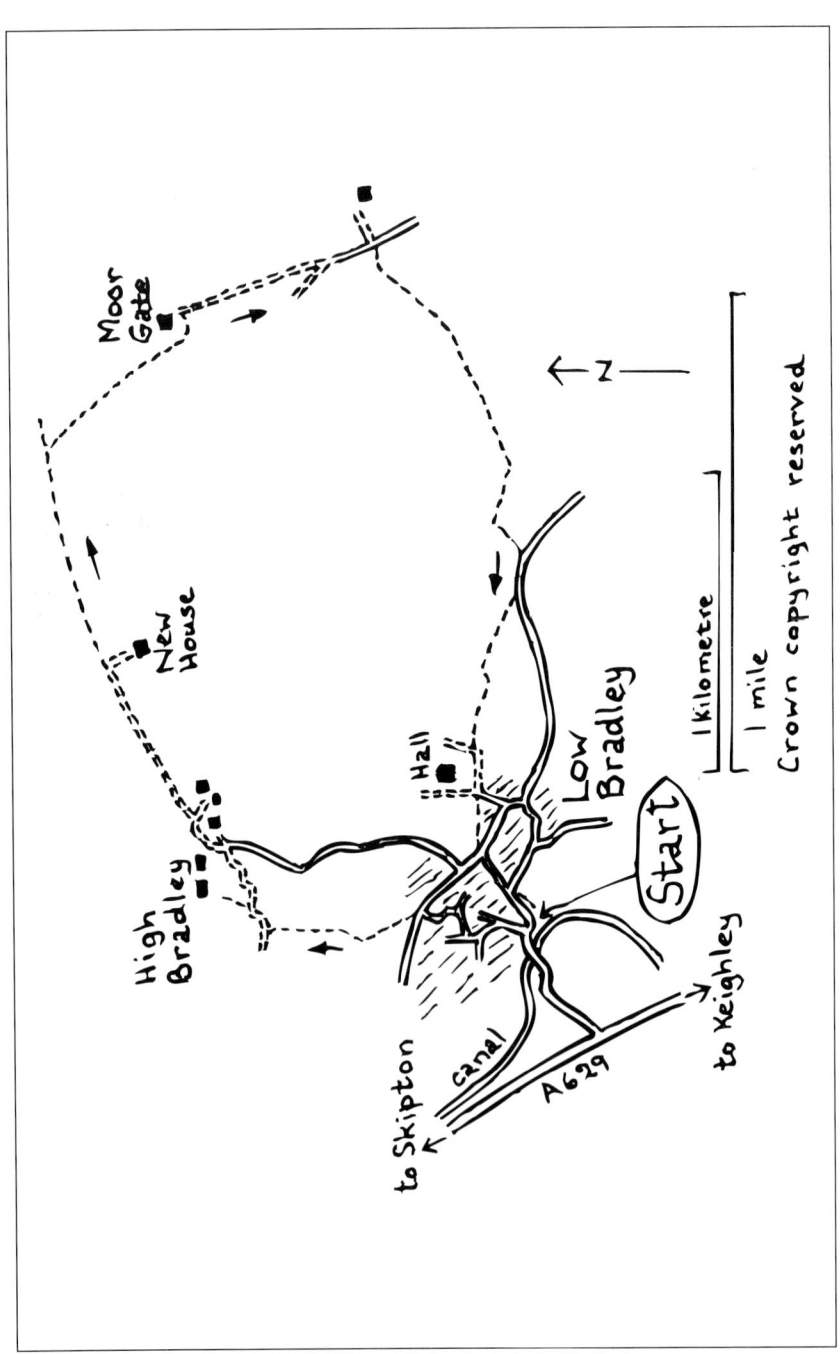

A short walk from the canalside car park in Low Bradley

South Pennines Outdoor Leisure Map. 4½ miles (7 km). Low and High Bradley are collectively known as Bradleys Both. Formerly most of the villagers were engaged in handloom weaving in their own homes, then in the 1860s spinning and weaving mills were opened. In the 1960s the new estate through which our walk starts almost doubled the size of the village. The countryside behind is one of pastoral tranquillity with superb views, which deserves to be better known. On this short stroll, keep pausing and looking around to enjoy the distant prospects.

Buses: *Keighley & District Travel (tel. 01535-603284) No.70/78 Keighley to Skipton pass the starting point, No. 66/68 Keighley to Skipton go along the A629; alight at Ings Lane and walk up it to the starting point.*

From the car park entrance walk up Ings Drive opposite. Ignore a fork right into Raines Drive, one left into Woodfield Drive, another one left into Aire Valley Drive, another left into Ings Drive (No Through Road), one right into Heath Crescent. The road swings to the left, then to the right and climbs to a T-junction (Skipton Road). Turn left but immediately after the last house on the right go through the stile on the right and walk up the field following the wall on your left. Where this wall turns left, bear slightly right up the field to a stile in the wall at the top. Cross this and bear slightly left up the next field to a stile near the top left hand corner. Cross this and walk forward, cutting the corner of the field, to the next stile by a gate on the right. Turn right along the grassy track.

Follow this walled lane to the road at High Bradley. On emerging through a gate onto this road, walk forward and you are faced by a fork: keep left. The road climbs and curves right and soon the tarmac surface ends. Keep left at the next fork and take the gently climbing track with a high wall to your right. The wall on the left ends at a gate, but the track continues, still with the wall to the right. Where the track bends right through a gate and drops to New House Farm, leave it and keep forward, still with the wall to your right. Go through the gate in the field corner, and now you have lost the wall on both sides. Keep forward on the track. Pass through the next gateway, and when the track forks, keep left, to pass through another gateway. Keep forward up the next field, now once more with a wall on your right.

Continue through one more field, but instead of going through the gate at the end of it cross the step-stile a few yards to the right of this. This is a fine viewpoint, and you may be surprised to see straight ahead in the distance Ilkley with the Cow and Calf and Otley Chevin. Having crossed the stile you find yourself in a field corner. Bear half right, diagonally across the middle of the field, and soon you will see that you are heading for a small barn. When you reach it, bear right between the redundant gateposts and continue down the edge of the field with a wall to your left. Beamsley Beacon comes into view away to the left. Cross the stile to the left of the gateway and keep following the wall on the left. Cross the stile in the field corner and follow the boundary wall of Moor Gate Farm on your left round until you reach the farm access road and turn right along this.

Follow this road until you reach the access road to the next farm on the left, High Bracken Hill. A few yards further on there is a gate on the right with a stile to the left of it. Cross this (it's none too easy!) and follow the wall on your right along to the gate into the next field. Go through and bear left along the wall on your left. About 50 yards from the far end of the field, which is narrowing, when you reach a gate on the left, cross right over the field to a stile in the wall on the opposite side. Over this turn left, again with a wall to your left. In a few yards you reach yet another superb viewpoint. When the wall turns left, keep straight down the field to the wall corner below and walk forward with this wall to your right.

You come to a stile in it, a stone step-stile surmounted by a high wooden fence, crossable only by olympic athletes. If you can cross it, do so, and turn left down the field with the wall to your left. Otherwise continue down by the wall, pass through the next gate ahead and keep on by the wall until you reach a gate in it. Go through and turn left and you are now back on the right of way. Go through the next gate and keep on by the wall on your left. The wall curves right and begins to drop more steeply. About 80 yards from the bottom corner of the field go through the gate in the wall on the left and bear half right across the field to a stile by the gate in the bottom corner out onto the road.

Turn right down the road, but only as far as the next gate on the right. Cross the stile beside it and bear left down the field parallel to the wall on your left, passing the end of a piece of wall jutting out into the field. Cross the stile in the bottom corner and continue down, now with a wall to your right, crossing two further stiles, before crossing a further stile in the wall ahead out onto a walled lane. Turn left along it, and when it opens out, follow the wall on the right to pass through a gate and continue down the lane. At the T-junction turn right for a detour to look at Low Bradley Old Hall, a superb house dated 1678, then return past the lane you have just come down and at the end of the next garden wall on the right turn right down College Court and pass to the left of the garages into an enclosed paved path. Cross a stile into a field and continue down, back into an enclosed path and down to Lidget Road. Cross this and continue down Rose Terrace opposite. Having passed Matthew Lane on the left, go into the playing fields on the left and turn right to follow their boundary wall to a footbridge into the car park from which you started.

A Walk through Carleton Glen

South Pennines Outdoor Leisure Map. 4 miles (6.2 km). Start and finish in Carleton in Craven. Pennine Motors service 211 leaves Skipton bus station on Monday-Saturday at 35 minutes past each hour for Carleton, and on Sundays at 14.40, 16.40 and 18.40. The journey takes 10 minutes. There is street parking for cars in Carleton. Dominant in the village is the large Victorian cotton mill, but the best building is Spence's Court, at the end of the village on the road to Skipton, almshouses founded in 1698 and built round three sides of a narrow courtyard. The walk has superb views.

Walk up the main street in Carleton and turn left up a track called The Wend. At the end cross the beck by the bridge on the left and follow the track through a farmyard and up through several fields. When the track ends cross the field to the trees and turn left, keeping the trees and the steep bank on your right. White marker posts point the way. At one of these posts the path descends into the glen. Cross a stile and the tiny beck and climb steeply up the facing slope. At the top of the steep part, turn left uphill with the ravine down to your left. The next stile is 10 yards to the right of the wall corner. Bear slightly right up the next large field to a gate in the top corner, then follow the fence on your right and the path drops steeply down to the next beck, which is crossed by stepping stones.

Bear left to the stile and climb steeply up the facing slope. Having reached the top of the steep part, turn left and walk parallel to the beck down below. Pass through the next wall where it has collapsed (the old stile is just to the right) and head for Gawthorpe House at the top of the next field. Don't forget to look back for the views! Cross a stile with the farm entrance opposite and turn left through a gate and down a track. It leads through a gateway and on up the next field, and where it peters out keep forward up the field to the gate in the top left hand corner. Keep forward up the next field, first with a fence, then with a wall to your right. Cross the stile at the top and turn right up the road.

There are superb views: Great Whernside, Buckden Pike, Ingleborough, Pen-y-Ghent are all visible. At the T-junction turn left and at the next road junction keep straight on. Look out for a clear track forking left through a large metal gate (there may be an arrow pointing to Tewit Cote) and follow it. Coming over the brow of the hill there is a fine view into Airedale and here you must look out for a grassy track forking left off the main one and leading to a gate. Don't go through the gate, a track which leads to Cononley, but turn left and cross the stile ahead. Now follow the wall on your right. The next stile is made redundant by a gap in the wall, and now the wall is on your left. Follow the path down into a dip, in which you cross the stile in the wall on the left. Walk downhill with the wall to your left to cross the next stile in the bottom corner.

Head towards the right hand end of Carleton Park farmhouse, but when you reach the wall bear left and follow it to a gate in the far corner of the field.

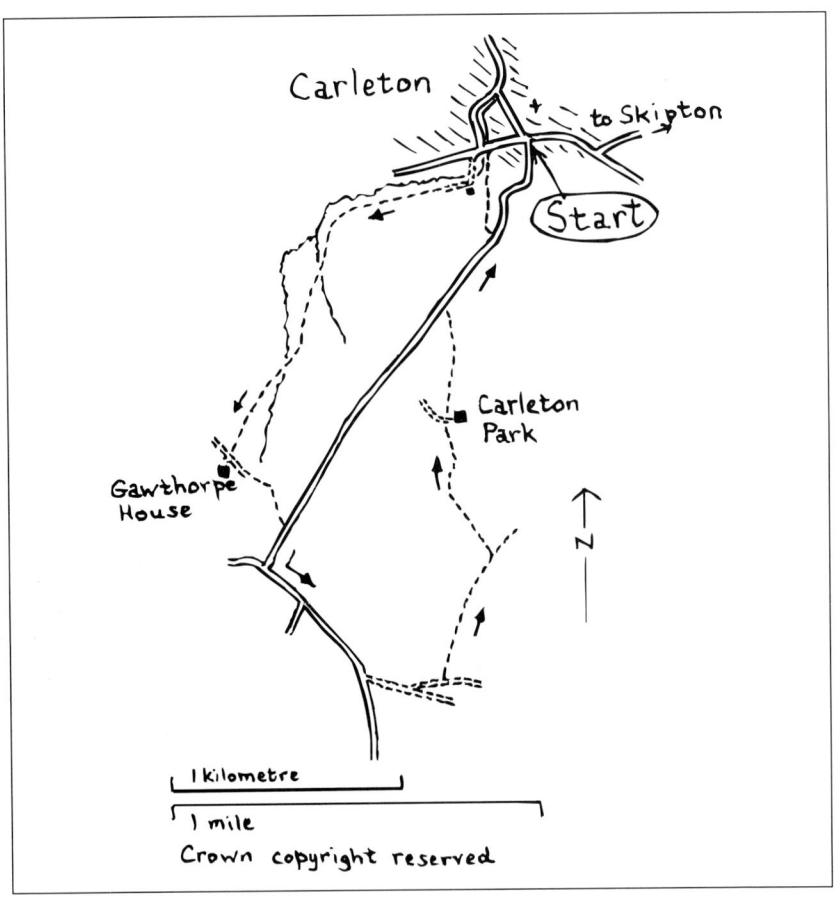

Cross the access drive and walk across the grass to the left hand of the two gates ahead. Now follow the wall on your right, but when it begins to curve slightly right, bear half left away from it to a stile in the far left hand corner of the field (the stiles around here are marked with white paint). Bear half left again to the next stile a few yards to the right of a gate, then turn right down the fenced path, and when it ends keep on with the wall on your right to a gated stile leading into a short lane. Turn left to the road and right along it.

Cross a stile on the left a few yards before a concrete bench and follow the left hand edge of the field to the next stile. Turn right with the wall to your right and follow it down to a wall corner, then straight down the field towards the new houses. Cross the stile, walk down the ginnel, straight over the end of the street and down the steps. This path leads back to the main street in Carleton.

A Walk from Skipton to Sharp Haw
Outdoor Leisure Map No.10 Yorkshire Dales Southern area. 10 miles (16 km). Field paths, heather moorland, woodland and a delightful viewpoint make this a favourite walk from Skipton, the "Gateway to the Dales".

Make your way to the top end of the Market Place, forking left at the War Memorial in front of the Parish Church along the road to Settle and Kendal, but where 100 yards further on the main road forks left along Water Street and the road to Grassington continues straight ahead, fork right up a narrower tarmac lane, soon forking left again by a house called "Fairview" (the right fork indicates "Private Road No Cars") up to a step-stile which you will see by a gate ahead.

Cross the stile and bear half-right up the field to the next stile a few yards to the left of a gate which you will soon see in the wall at the top (good view back over Skipton). Over the stile keep straight forward down the next field on a clear path, parallel to the wall and wood about 60 yards away on your right, to the next stile. Cross straight over the lane and slant left up to the Skipton bypass. Cross this busy road with care to the stile opposite and walk straight forward across the next field to another stile which leads onto the golf course. Again keep straight forward, keeping a lookout for flying missiles, across the golf course to the far side, where you pick up a short stretch of wall: keep to the left of it and it will lead you to a stile in the corner. Continue with the wall to your right to cross the stile by the facing gate at the far end of the field, then bear slightly left to the fence/hedge on the left, which you follow down to a stile and a tarmac lane. Turn left along this.

At the main road cross straight over to the stile opposite and keep forward with the hedge to your left, but where the hedge kinks right then left again bear half-right across the corner of the field to the next stile by a power line pole. Now again follow the hedge/fence on your left to the next stile, then keep forward along the minor road. It bends right, then left, then right again; a yard or two after this bend go through the gate on the left marked Private Road (but signposted Bridleway to Flasby).

Follow the track through a gate in a fence, ignore a minor track forking right and keep forward to pass through a gate in a wall. Follow the track for another 100 yards, then fork slightly right off it by a bridleway sign along a grassy track. Pass through a gate and follow the clear path all the way to the summit of Sharp Haw, which lies directly in front of you. At 1171' (357m) this delectable summit is a fine viewpoint. From the trig point keep forward along the summit ridge for 60 yards, before forking right to pass through a narrow gateway in a wall. From

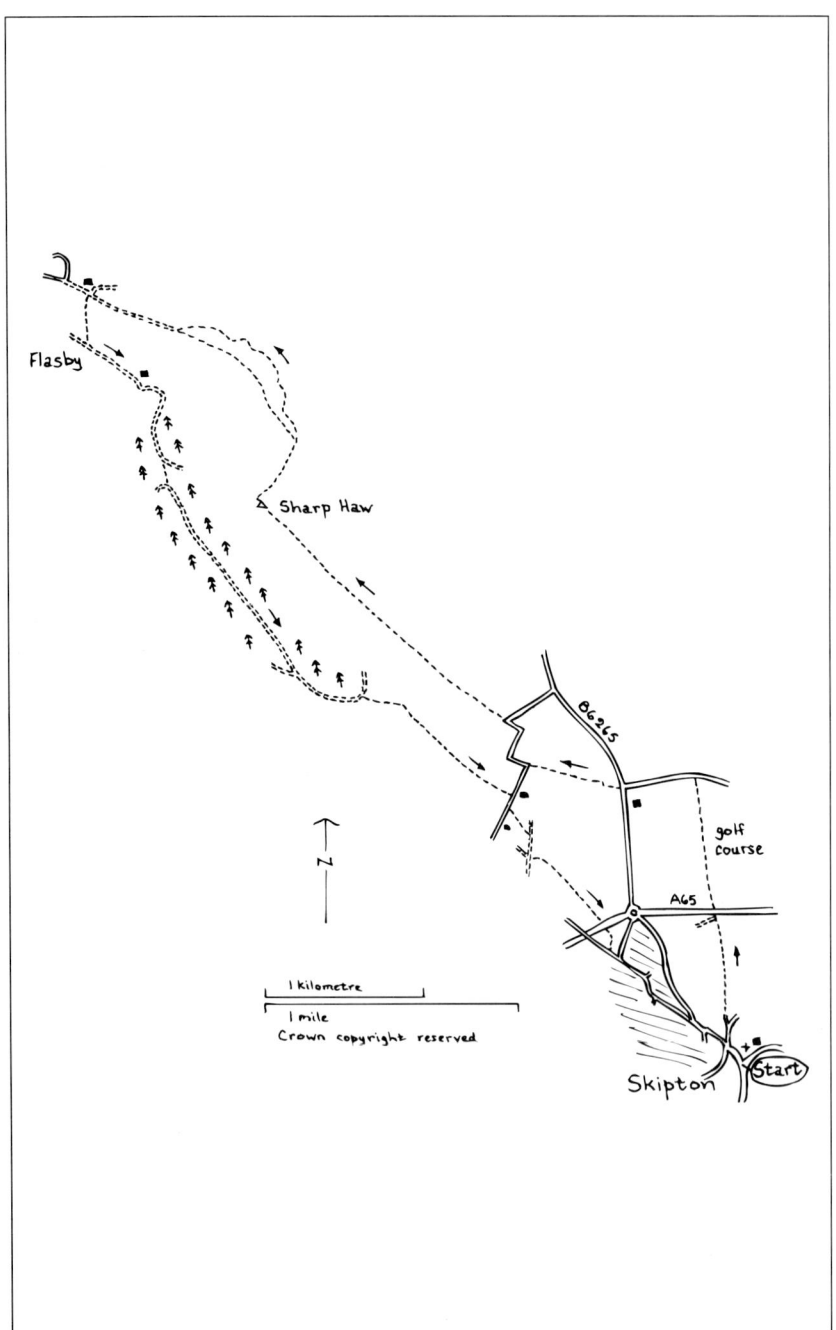

here a clear path leads forward across the moor to a gate in the wall opposite. Now ignore the path straight ahead up onto Rough Haw and bear half-left along another clear path.

You can follow this very clear path all the way down to a gate in the bottom corner of the moor, from there following a wall on your left to another gate and then resuming the walk description at + below, but the actual right of way follows a more interesting route, although it can be very wet in places. If you want to try it, fork right off the clear path about 30 yards after you cross the brow of the hill and start to descend - the spot has a marker post with a blue top - on a much narrower path through the bracken. It contours and actually climbs a little before dropping to another marker post and then slanting down towards the wall on the right and descending the hillside about 30 yards from this wall. Don't be tempted left, keep straight down, pass another marker post, over some wet parts, to cross a side beck, then bear half-left to reach a gate in the facing wall about 150 yards to the right of the gate in the bottom corner of the moor. Bear half-left across the large field to a gate in the far corner near a power line pole.

+ Follow the track to Flasby. There you pass through a kissing-gate, ignore a track forking right (signposted to Rylstone) and keep forward, but opposite the farm on the right take the ascending fenced track on the left (signposted Stirton). It levels out, but eventually bears left and begins to climb gently again. Pass to the right of a cottage, cross a small stone bridge, go through a gate and keep on the track, which begins to climb again and swings left, then right, to enter the woods through a kissing-gate. Follow the track until it bends left uphill then levels out again: shortly after this watch out for a fork with a footpath sign pointing right to Bog Lane. Here fork right onto a narrow path which leads forward to reach a forest road on a bend. Bear left along this, uphill (another signpost to Bog Lane).

Now follows a longish woodland tramp. Eventually you are joined by another forest road from the right, and soon an unplanted area on the right gives you a nice view to the Leeds and Liverpool Canal. The track begins to ascend again and bears left. On this bend look out for a narrow path branching right at right-angles to the track and descending to a stile which you will see in a facing wall. From the stile look straight forward: a row of trees ahead marks a deep ravine, and you must pass round the lefthand end of this ravine to a gate which is behind the trees. Cross the stile beside this gate and follow the wall on your left; where it turns sharp right cross the stile by the gate in the corner and keep forward parallel to the fence on your left to a step-stile in it about 100 yards down. Now turn right and follow the fence on your right down and then left to reach a gate in a facing wall near the next corner (NOT the gate on the right). Keep forward along the righthand edge of the next field to a gate-stile onto the road and turn right.

In 100 yards cross a ladder-stile on the left and bear slightly right to pass between two large trees and through a kissing-gate into a lane. Tarn Caravan Park is ahead. Turn right down the lane, but just before the drive from Thorlby House comes in from the right find a curious stile on the left which leads into a fenced path along the bottom edge of the caravan park. Cross a ladder-stile into a field and bear half-left across the corner of this to a step-stile by a gate, then half-right up the next large field, passing to the right of a power line pole and under the power lines towards a tree by a fence corner ahead, then keep forward on the same line across the corner of the field, heading towards another large tree, and bear left down with the hedge/fence on your right to a stile in the bottom corner of the field. Walk straight over the next field to the stile opposite and descend the bank to cross the bypass once more with great care, climb steeply up the bank on the other side, over the stile and half-right across the field, past a power line pole to the stile a few yards beyond it. Turn left along the road to return to the centre of Skipton.

3.3 Skipton to Gargrave

Start and finish at Skipton Station. I suggest that motorists use one of the free car parks in Gargrave and walk by the towpath to Skipton, returning to Gargrave by the Airedale Way. Once a busy market town, after the opening of the canal Gargrave became an important transport centre. Until the 1930s the cotton industry was a major employer, and two of the old mills have been converted to residential use. The Johnson & Johnson factory which manufactures medical supplies is situated in a third. Refreshments can be had at pubs and cafés in Skipton and Gargrave.

From the main entrance to the station cross the main road and, ignoring the road going left signposted to Carleton and Lothersdale walk straight up a narrower road to the canal. Don't cross the bridge, but **turn left along the towpath.**

Shortly after leaving the last houses of Skipton behind and passing under the A629 the towpath joins a road by Niffany Bridge, with Niffany Farm across the canal. Keep along with the railings on your right, but when the towpath resumes through a gate, stay on the road and cross the railway, walking with care as there is a lot of traffic and no footway or usable verge. When the road curves right to the A59, fork left off it past a metal gate along the former road to cross the Aire by the old stone bridge. At the end of the path cross the main road and then the stile opposite and walk left for a few yards to the next stile. Bear slightly left across the next large field, aiming for two large trees close together on the far side.

As you draw nearer, you see that the trees are in fact in the next field, but before them there is a stile in a short section of wall on the right. Cross this and keep your line over the next, enormous field, parallel to the railway over to your right and gradually drawing closer to the wall which is the left hand boundary of the field, visible in the distance. *The hill over to the right is Sharp Haw, with Crag Wood below it.* **Cross the stile in the far left hand corner of the field and continue with a wall to your left.** *To your right in this field is a large old meander of the Aire, probably cut off when the river was straightened to enable the railway to be built.* **Cross the stile in the next field corner and turn right to follow the wall on your right down and pass through the tunnel under the railway. Turn left along the wall parallel to the railway.** *As you breast a rise, Gargrave appears ahead.* **Go through the gate in the next field corner and keep on by the wall.**

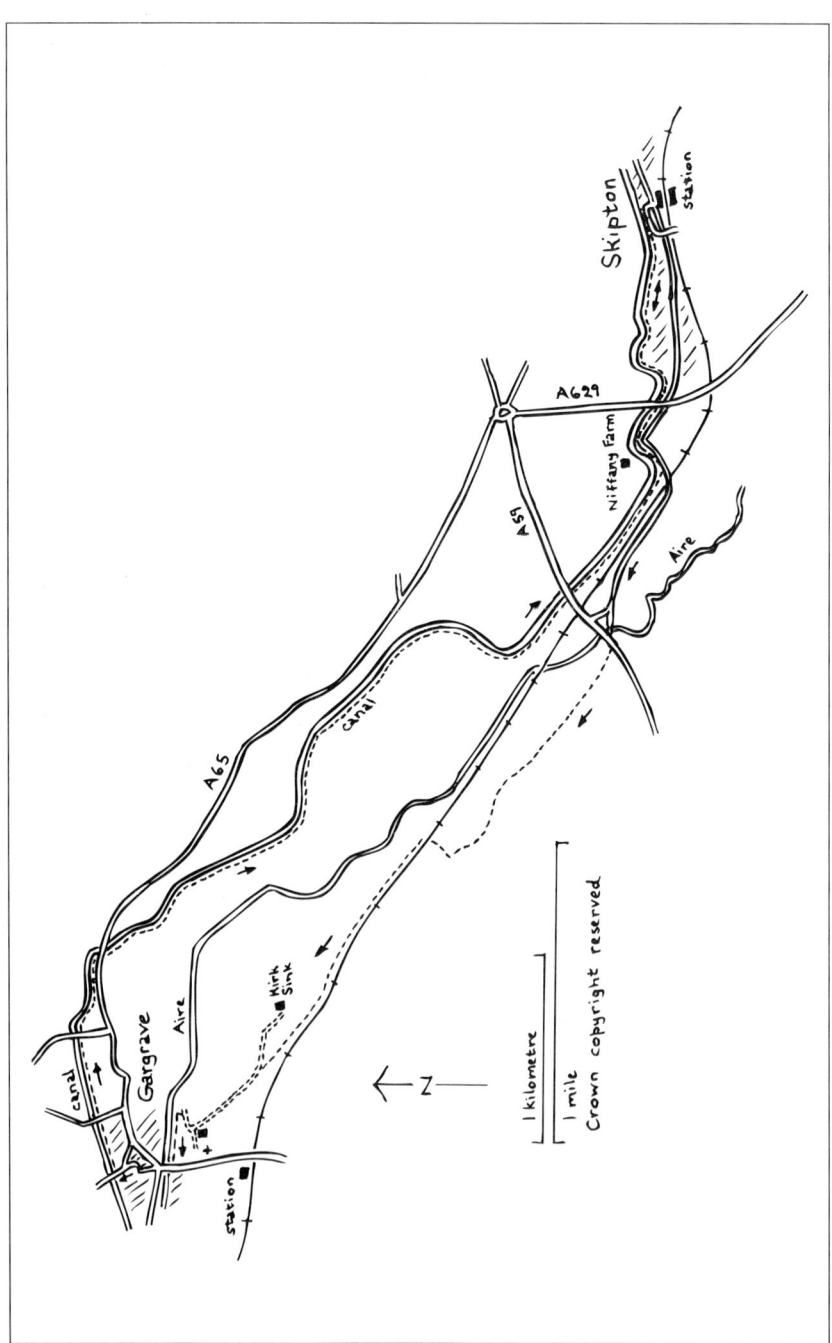

Before you reach the next corner, bear slightly right away from the wall to follow a line of old trees to a wall. The stile is missing here, but a short distance to the left the wall has collapsed and can easily be climbed. Continue along to the left of the line of old trees, in the remains of a green way. *The large factory half right belongs to Johnson & Johnson.* When the trees end, go left on the track, which is heading for another tunnel under the railway. But before you reach this fork right to a kissing-gate and follow the fence on your right along until you reach a gate in it. Pass through and turn left to the next stile a few yards further on. Now stay beside the fence on your left to climb to the crest of the hill. *Looking right from here, in the field to the left of the house called Kirk Sink the map shows the site of a Roman villa.*

Looking half right you will see a lane heading to the houses of Gargrave. Drop half right and join this lane over a stile. Walk along it towards the houses. Cross a cattle grid into the yard of Low Green Farm and walk straight on, passing to the left of some stables, then leave the yard and turn right along the track. When you draw level with a bench and stepping stones over the river, leave the track, walk to the riverside and turn left along it. There are more benches, and this is a lovely spot for a picnic. As you come closer to Gargrave Bridge you join a tarmac lane which leads up to the next road (Church Street). The Airedale Way crosses straight over and along the tarmac lane opposite. *The Mason's Arms is a short distance left along Church Street.*

But most walkers will want to turn right and follow the Pennine Way over the bridge and into Gargrave. Here there are cafés, pubs and if you go right from the end of the bridge public toilets. To return to Skipton cross the main road and take the minor road opposite, by the side of the Dalesman Café. When the road turns right after Gargrave Village Hall, keep straight on up a narrower road, which soon leads to the canal. A signpost here says Skipton 4¾, Leeds 33¾. Turn right along the towpath. Just before the concrete bridge which carries the A65 over the canal you cross Eshton Beck by Holme Aqueduct. Eventually you pass by a gate onto a road and rejoin your outward route. Walk along the road, rejoin the towpath beside Niffany Bridge and follow it back to the swing bridge where you turn right down the lane to return to Skipton Station.

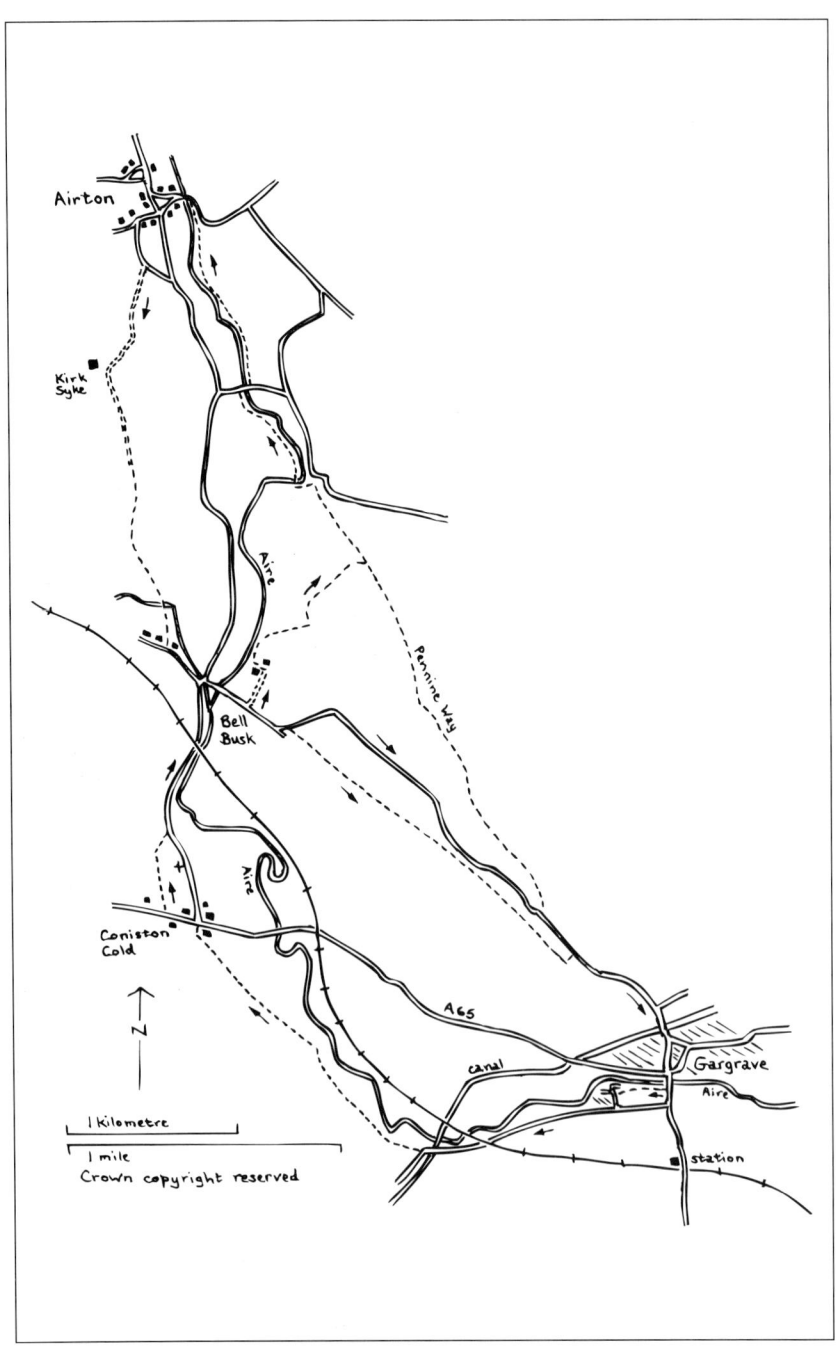

Stage 4 Gargrave to Malham Tarn (11½ miles, 18.3 km)

This stage can be divided into two shorter walks:
4.1 Gargrave to Airton (10½ miles, 17 km)
4.2 Airton to Malham Tarn (12 miles, 19.2 km)

4.1 Gargrave to Airton

Start and finish at Gargrave Station. Motorists should park in one of the free car parks in Gargrave. Refreshments can be had at pubs and cafés in Gargrave. The Airedale Way joins the Pennine Way on Eshton Moor and the two follow the same route to Airton.

From the station walk up the road to the village, passing the Mason's Arms, and immediately before the bridge over the Aire fork left down a tarmac lane. **The lane soon narrows to a footpath and follows a mill race. Join another tarmac lane and keep forward along it. At the next T-junction turn left uphill, and then fork right and right again along the next road. There is no footway, but not much traffic either. You cross a bridge where Crossber Beck joins the Aire, and for a short distance the river is close by on the right. Pass under the railway. The road crosses the canal at Priest Holme Bridge, and looking right from the bridge you can see where the canal crosses the Aire on an aqueduct. The road turns sharp left after the bridge, but the Way keeps straight forward over the stile by the gate.**

Walk along the top of the bank, soon picking up a fence on the right, which you follow to the corner of the field, where there is a stile in it. Cross this and turn left for a few yards, then right over a slab bridge. Bear half left across the field, passing close to the river where this makes a bend, then leaving it again and following the same line on over the field to a gate on the far side. Go through and walk straight up the slope. Pass to the right of the fenced plantation and from it keep forward down the line of an old hedge. Near the bottom bear half left to a stile in the wall ahead. Cross it and bear half left again up the next field to a gap stile which is already visible. Walk straight across the middle of the next large field to cross a stile by the left hand of the gates on the far side. Now you follow a wall/fence/hedge on your right. Go through the gate ahead and keep following the wall. Pass through the next gate and keep forward, now on a track. It leads through another gate and down to the A65 in Coniston Cold.

Ignore the road opposite, signposted to Bell Busk and Malham, and turn left along the main road for about 150 yards to a signposted stile by a gate on the right. Over this walk straight up the field to the next stile by another gate. Cross the track and continue with the hedge to your right. When you reach a paved path crossing yours, a private footpath from Coniston Hall to the church, go through the gate on the right, then bear half left to pass the corner of the wood and reach the road through a gate. Turn left along the road. Soon you are close to the Aire again. Pass under the railway (for the last time!). *Just after passing the Mill House, Otterburn Beck flows into the Aire.* At the next junction turn right to cross Otterburn Beck, then immediately fork right again along the lane, which soon crosses the Aire.

Pass Aire Bridge House and take the next farm access road on the left over a cattle-grid. Follow it up to the farm and turn left to pass behind the farmhouse, between it and some stables. Enter a small field and cross it half right to a metal gate. Go through and turn right along the wall, parallel to the river on your left. *Here you enter the Yorkshire Dales National Park.* When the wall turns sharp right, go with it, pass through a gate and keep on up the wallside, passing a barn, to another gate. Go through and bear half left along a grassy track which leads you up to the wall at the top of the slope. *There is a pleasant view of Airedale to the left.* Follow the wall along, go through the second gateway in it and bear half left over the next large field to a gate in the wall.

Pass through the gated stile beside the large gate *(a few yards to the right is a Pennine Way sign, as you here join the Pennine Way)*, from which there is a fine view up Airedale, with Newfield Hall prominent in the middle distance. Walk half-left to the bottom corner of this large field, joining on the way the clear path trodden out by Pennine Way walkers. Having reached the corner, keep on down with a fence and road to the right and a wall to the left, and when faced by a beck, go through the stile in this wall and follow the path along, to cross the Aire by a footbridge. The path crosses the field parallel to the river and enters a wood through a small gate, but just in front of a large tree a stile on the right leads back down to the river. The path is now parallel to the wall on the left, but just before the wall makes a sharp turn left, cross the sleeper bridge on the right and walk straight over the field to a stile onto the road a few yards to the left of Newfield Bridge.

Turn right and cross the bridge, but a few yards further on cross the stile on the left and bear left to the river bank, which is followed until you reach a stile in the next facing wall. From here one path keeps close to the river, another stays parallel to the wall on the right. Both lead at the far end of the field to two stiles close together. Now bear left, with the wall to your left, and follow it round to the next stile. Walk straight over the middle of the next field towards the houses of Airton. A stile leads out onto the road by Airton Bridge. The Airedale Way continues along the lane directly opposite.

To return to Gargrave turn left over the bridge, passing Airton Mill, once a water-driven corn mill in the possession of Fountains Abbey, in the 19th century spinning cotton, now converted into flats, into this charming village. Notice the old squatter's cottage and the remains of the stocks on the green. Keep left at the fork by the green and cross straight over the main road to follow the road signposted to Otterburn and Hellifield. At the top of the slope fork left along the road signposted rather illegibly to Bell Busk, but soon fork right off it along a lane leading to Kirk Syke Farm. After some distance ignore the entrance into the farm, soon afterwards passing to the left of a barn, and the lane is now grassier. Soon after you pass through a gate the enclosed lane ends. Keep forward on the track by the wall on the right. Pass through another gate, then continue forward to the right of a barn and on to the next gate visible ahead.

After it the field boundary is on your left. Shortly after the fence meets a wall, go through the gate on the left and keep the fence on your right to a barn. Pass to the left of the barn and follow the track, which first crosses a bridge over Otterburn Beck, all the way to the road at Bell Busk. *Here you leave the Yorkshire Dales National Park again.* Turn left along the road. At the next junction turn left over the bridge across Otterburn Beck (you have been here before!), along the road signposted to Airton and Malham, but immediately after the bridge take the right fork, along a road signed as Unsuitable for Motors, soon crossing the Aire.

This time ignore the farm access road on the left, and keep forward. When you reach a fork turn sharp left, ignoring a cattle-grid and the access drive to Hespber Farm, and now you you have a choice of route to return to Gargrave. You can either follow this track all the way, which is the easier alternative, or you can use a pleasant path through the fields. But be warned, the path goes through some enormous fields and in the summer you may come across a bull in one or other of them!

If you choose to follow the track, you have the opportunity to make a short detour to the trig point on Haw Crag, a superb viewpoint for a large section of the route of the Airedale Way, although to reach it involves committing a minor trespass. So when the track turns sharp right, go through the gate ahead and follow the track uphill, leaving it when you can bear left round the rim of the old quarry to the summit. Having enjoyed the view, retrace your steps to the lane and continue back to Gargrave.

If you decide to return by the fields, go through the first gate on the right off the track after you have turned left at the entrance to Hespber Farm and follow the clear grassy track, almost a hollow way, over the field. Near the far side ignore the gap stile ahead and bear left to pass the wall corner, then continue across the field to cross a stile in a short section of wall ahead. Walk over the next field to the ladder stile opposite (the whole of this path is fairly consistently waymarked with blue arrows instead of yellow ones) and now bear slightly left to the corner of the wood ahead. In the corner of the field cross the stile by the gate on the left and walk along the bottom of the wood to a gap stile (where there is a warning about a bull). Follow the fence on the left along this enormous field. After it kinks left and there is a gate in it, the fence borders the track, our easier alternative. Omit the kink and continue straight ahead at this point, gradually bearing right away from the fence to pass through a gate in the facing wall at the end of the field about 60 yards to the right of the field corner, then head straight over another enormous field.

As you come over the rise you will see below a fence corner: make for this and walk along to the right of the fence. Cross a stile in the field corner and continue forward till you come to a gate in the fence on the left. Go through and follow the track up to the lane. Turn right down it to return to Gargrave.

Having crossed the canal into Gargrave, to return to the station, walk down through the village to the main road, cross it and go right for a few yards to the minor road on the left which crosses the Aire.

4.2 Airton to Malham Tarn

Users of public transport start and finish in Airton. There is an infrequent bus service (Pennine 210) from Skipton to Malham via Gargrave and Airton. As one wants to avoid cluttering up the lovely village of Airton with parked cars, I suggest that motorists park at Street Gate (GR 903 656) and do the return half of the walk first, starting at [#] below. Refreshments are available at The Victoria, Kirkby Malham (10 minutes from the route) and at pubs and cafés in Malham. There is often a van serving teas and ices on the road just south of Malham Tarn.

From Airton village follow the road down to the river. **On the far side of the bridge turn left down the track, cross the stile into the field and walk parallel to the river. Cross the next stile and the footbridge and follow the clear path forward. Keep straight on across the field, pass a small brick shed and continue across the next field, soon bearing left to cross a stone footbridge and reach a stile in a short section of wall. Cross this and the wooden footbridge beyond and turn right, heading for a wall corner. The path passes to the left of this and you follow the wall to two gates close together. Keep on by the river, but shortly before you draw level with a ruined stone barn on the right, bear slightly right away from the river and pass through a kissing-gate at the far end of the field. Follow the river to Hanlith, with Hanlith Hall prominent ahead.**

Go up the steps beside the bridge. *Hanlith is up to the right, Kirkby Malham a ten minute walk along the road to the left, and here you leave the Pennine Way.* **Turn left over the bridge, then immediately right along the access road to Scalegill Mill.** *The mill was originally a corn mill, but the present buildings date from 1795, when the mill was used for spinning cotton; it has now been made into holiday homes.* **Go through the kissing-gate to the left of the entrance and pass to the left of the buildings. Now you follow the old mill leat, which you cross twice at a point where it has been made into a watering place for animals. The path then passes the mill reservoir, and rounding a bend you catch a first sight of Malham and the Cove. Cross the stile and follow the wall on the right.** *Just before the next stile to the right of the path a spring issues from the ground, and just beyond the stile there is another. This is Aire Head, the official source of the River Aire.* **Now follow the cairns across the field to the ladder-stile in the far wall. Keep forward to cross a footbridge and another ladder-stile, with Malham Beck to your right, then on over the next field to a ladder-stile just to the left of a gate, out onto the**

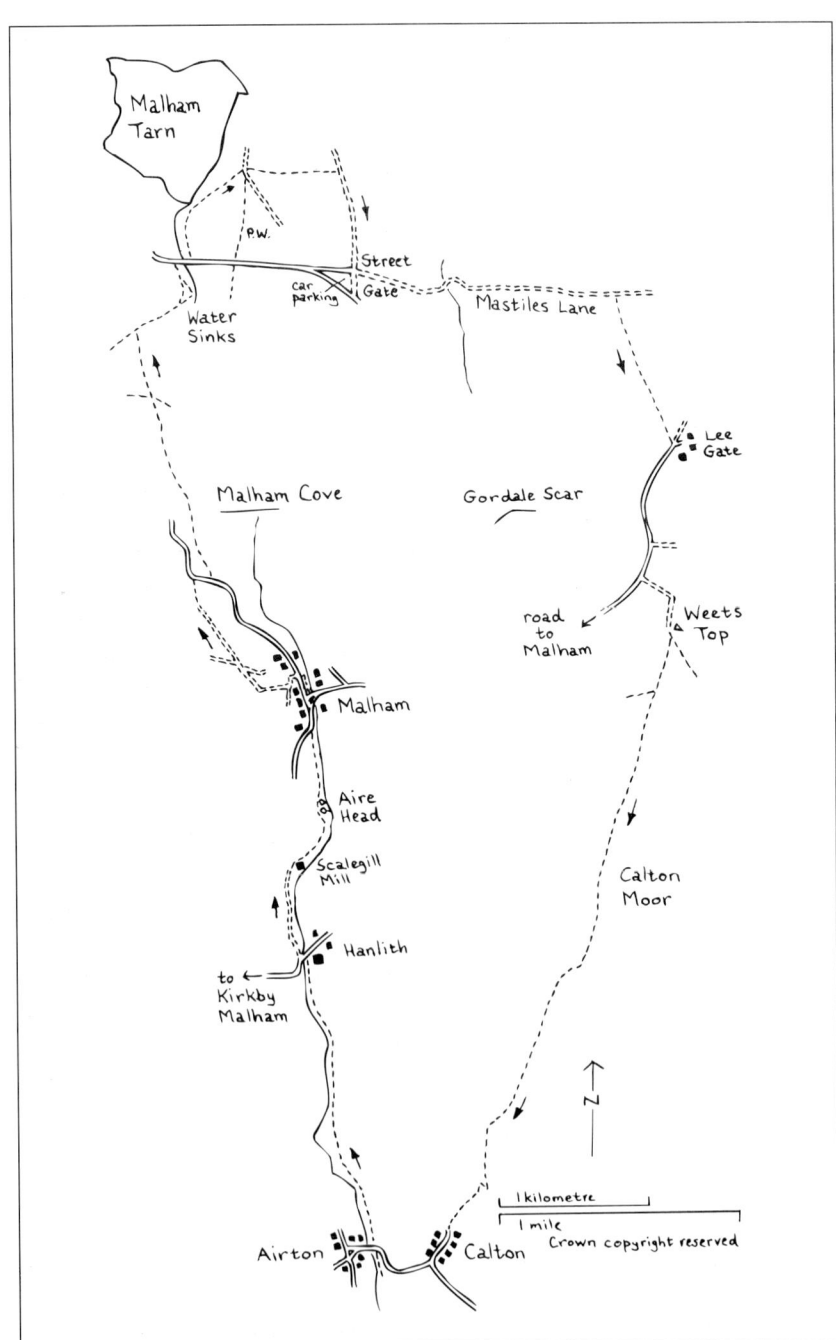

road in Malham. The National Park Centre (with toilets) is to the left, we turn right through the village.

Now let's find a quiet route to the Tarn! **Keep left when the road forks** *(there are more toilets on the left here),* **but in a few yards by the telephone kiosk turn right then immediately left through a small gate to follow the path through the wood. Emerge by another gate onto the road and cross to the signposted bridleway opposite. This walled lane leads up to a T-junction. Turn left for 30 yards, then right when the track forks. The track climbs and bears right. At the next fork, just past the Water Treatment Works, keep right.** *There are good views to the Cove over the wall on the right.* **At the end of the walled lane go through the gate and keep forward on the track to a gate on the far side of the field out onto the road. Turn right for 200 yards, then cross a stile on the left signposted Dean Moor.**

Walk across the field to the stile in the wall opposite, *with a lovely view down to the Cove,* **then straight up the next field on a faint grassy path. But having passed through the first group of windswept trees bear half left up to a track and keep forward along it to the next (ladder-) stile. Cross the corner of the next field to a wooden step stile. A clear path leads forward to cross the next wall by another ladder-stile, then cross the next field to the next stile,** *where you enter National Trust land (Ewe Moor).* **From the stile keep straight forward, pass through a broken wall, join a track and follow it forward, but when you see the next ladder-stile half right ahead, bear right off the track and pass between two limestone pavements, then turn right down by the wall to the stile.**

Cross the stile *(leaving N.T. land again)* **and keep forward on a faint path. Drop to cross a ladder-stile** *(N.T. land again!)* **and turn left (signposted Water Sinks and Malham Tarn) up the slope of Dean Moor Hill.** *Now you are among spacious limestone uplands.* **When you reach a clear cross track, turn right along it. When you cross the brow and Malham Tarn comes into view left, bear half right off the track to Water Sinks,** *where the beck which flows from the Tarn goes underground, to emerge as the River Aire at Aire Head.*

Follow the beck along, soon bearing half left away from it on a clear path leading to a footpath sign. Here you rejoin the track: turn right along it to a kissing-gate out onto the road. Turn right, cross the beck, go through a gate and when you reach a footpath sign on each side of the road, turn left through a popular car parking area and follow the broad grassy track out the other side

(NOT the path heading off further right through the tree stumps!). This track leads to Malham Tarn at Tarn Foot, where the beck flowing out is the real start of the River Aire, and journey's end.

To return to Airton, keep along with the Tarn to your left and you will soon hit a clear path bearing right away from it towards a wood. Pass to the right of the wood, then make for the right hand end of another small wood on the far side of an access road (NOT the gate some way to the left of it). Walk along the right hand edge of this wood, and when it ends keep forward to the wall and continue with the wall to your left. Great Close Scar and Hill are over to your left. Shortly after passing another small wood, Great Close Plantation, turn right along a farm access road and follow it to the next junction, Street Gate. Turn left [#] through the gate (signposted Grassington 6½) along Mastiles Lane.

The track drops and you cross Gordale Beck by a clapper bridge. Climbing the other side, according to the map you pass through the site of a Roman camp. Follow the track until you reach a gate in a cross wall. Go through - Mastiles Lane now becomes enclosed - but immediately go through another gate on the right and follow the wall on your right. Cracoe Pinnacle on Barden Moor comes into view. Follow the wall until a gate in the next cross wall leads you out onto Smearbottoms Lane, with the ugly sprawl of Lee Gate Farm to the left. Turn right along the road. Ignore the first walled lane you reach on the left, but turn up the second (signposted to Calton). As you climb look back for a fine view over Malhamdale to Kirkby Fell. At the top of the lane is Weets Cross.

Go through the gate. The trig point on Weets Top is just to the left, a superb all-round viewpoint. Take the right fork (signposted Calton) and follow the track parallel to the wall on the right all the way down (there is one cross wall with stile on the way) to where the wall turns right and you keep forward along the track. A deep ravine develops to your left and soon you drop quite steeply and pass through two gates in quick succession into a wooded area. When you reach Calton, keep forward along the road. At the junction on the far side of the hamlet continue downhill to Airton.

DOWN RIVER TO WOODLESFORD AND CASTLEFORD

Pathfinder 683 (Leeds), 692 (Dewsbury), 693 (Castleford & Pontefract). 6 miles (9½ km) to Woodlesford, 11¼ miles (17 km) to Castleford; A surprisingly attractive walk of great variety and much historical and wildlife interest; there is an opportunity to visit the Tetley Brewery Wharf Visitor Centre, The Royal Armouries Museum and the Thwaite Mills Industrial Museum. The walk is of course almost entirely level. Much of the route is part of the Trans Pennine Trail and is waymarked as such.

The walk, which is linear, starts at Leeds Station and the return is by train from either Woodlesford or Castleford (Hallam or Pontefract Lines). It would be possible to leave a car at Woodlesford Station, Woodlesford Lock or in Castleford, take the train to Leeds and walk back to the car.

On emerging from Leeds Station walk straight over the pedestrian crossing to a small white tower building with a sign saying Way Out Bishopgate, go down the steps and turn right, but immediately cross the main road by the pedestrian crossing and turn right to follow the road under the station. Pass the Hilton Hotel, then cross the end of Sovereign Street and continue over Victoria Bridge, then turn left along the riverside path past the Asda headquarters. It leads out onto Water Lane. Pass to the left of the Georgian Old Red Lion (Sam Smith), cross the main roads by the pedestrian crossings and walk straight forward along Dock Street to the right of the old offices of the Aire and Calder Navigation, now the North East Regional Office of British Waterways, noting the triangular red brick Leeds Bridge House, built around 1880.

Bear left along the cobbled Navigation Walk and soon go right along a pavement through a new housing development, which makes effective use of as much of the old warehouses as possible. Ignore a stout wooden footbridge and reach the river bank again. Follow it to the Tetley Brewery Wharf Centre. Keep by the river to Crown Point Bridge, pass under it and follow the broad paved footpath up to turn left over the bridge over the entrance to Clarence Dock, built around 1840, then pass to the left of the Royal Armouries Museum and to the right of Leeds Lock, built in 1822 and still manually operated. Continue on along the riverside path.

Pass under the green girder bridge (South Accommodation Road) and immediately turn right and climb the steps to the road. Turn right over the bridge and immediately beyond it turn right again to cross the grass and enter a gravel footpath. When this ends keep forward along the track, but where this widens to a tarmac open space just before a bridge

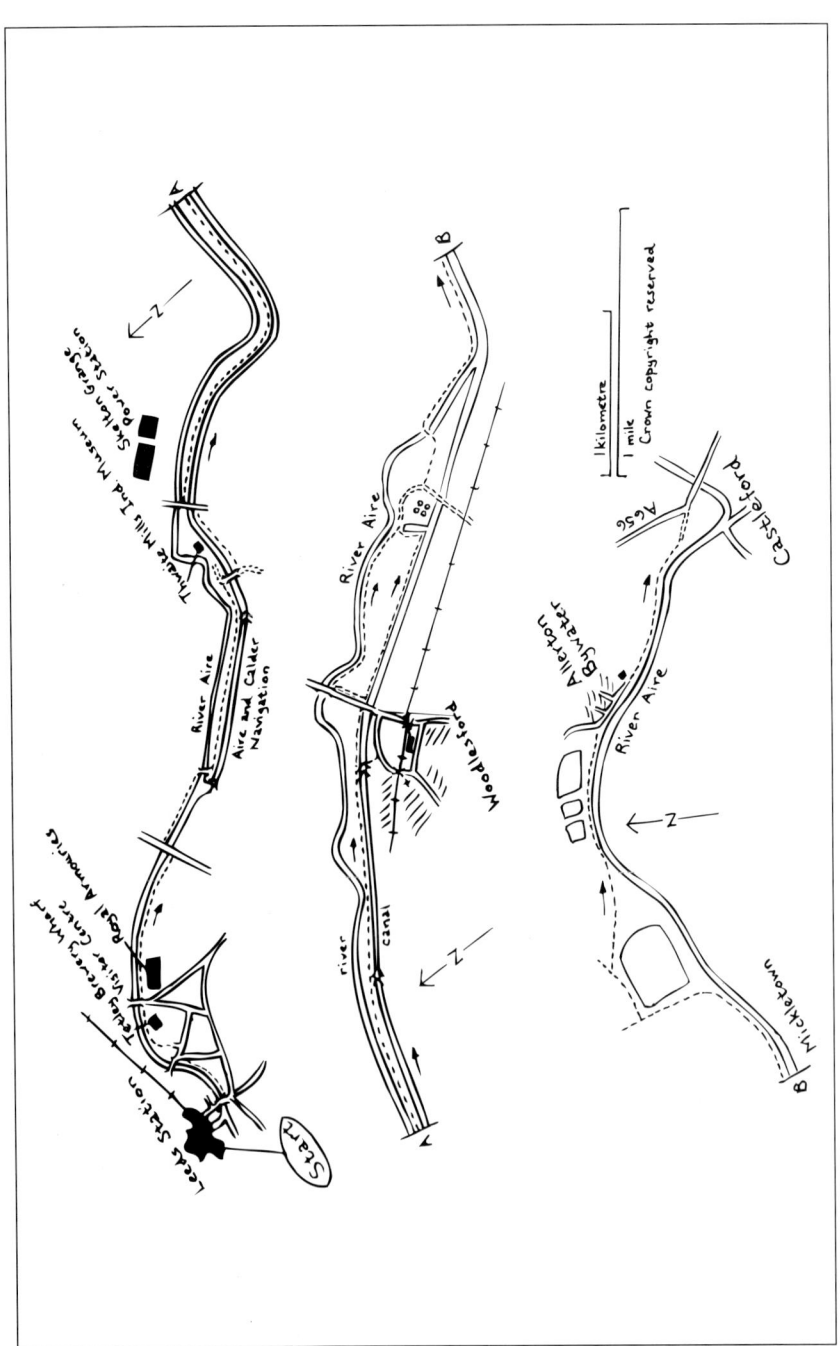

over the river, find the paved footpath in the righthand corner which passes under the bridge and follows a fence and pipeline along by the river. Cross the river by the next footbridge, turn left down the steps (Knostrop Flood Lock is to the right) and follow the path between the river and the canal.

Pass the next lock by a weir and the remains of a railway bridge, and in a short distance keep right at a fork along a narrower footpath. Look out for a flight of steps on the right (ignore them and keep on along the path if you want to visit Thwaite Mills) leading up to a road, and turn right to cross the canal. When the road curves right turn left to pass through wooden bollards and a metal barrier. Soon there is a lovely view over the canal to Thwaite Mills. Pass under the next concrete road bridge and follow the path as it bears right and climbs the steps to the road. Turn right over the bridge, but as soon as you have crossed the canal (and before you cross the river) go through a gate in the white metal railing on the right and descend the steps, there turning right along the path once more between the river and the canal. The next tree-lined section is perhaps the loveliest on the entire route. The large power station to the left is Skelton Grange.

Pass through a gateway under a pylon onto a track. A short distance before a concrete bridge over the canal keep right at a fork and follow the path under the bridge, then continue by the canal. Looking left there is a fine view to Temple Newsam in the distance. Pass Fishpond Lock and follow the path all the way to Woodlesford Lock. If you wish to finish the walk at Woodlesford, cross the canal by the farther set of lock gates and follow the track away from the canal into Woodlesford. Turn right at the next road, ignoring New Farmers Hill, and follow it up and over the railway bridge, then immediately turn left for the station. For Castleford keep on the path with the canal to your right.

Pass under the A642, and now you have a choice. Either continue along by the canal until the track bears left beside a canal basin, passes through a metal barrier and reaches a cross track where you turn right, or if you wish to include a short stretch of riverside path, about 100 yards after the road bridge turn sharp left along a track to the road. Turn right here over a stile and down a flight of steps to a new footpath which runs below the road embankment to join the track signposted to the right as the Leeds Country Way. Pass to the right of a derelict brick building, then bear right across a stile and walk along the river bank. Cross another stile and keep forward along a shaly path with a wood to the right. The path widens to a track and reaches a metalled track. Keep forward along it. Now the two routes have rejoined.

Pass a high hide and follow the path down to a car park, walk through this and continue along the road. Just round the first bend take the permissive bridleway signposted on the left. At a large tarmac area turn left to cross the river by a new bridge and turn right along the perimeter fence of the opencast coal workings. Keep by this fence, passing two more new bridges (as you approach the second, Ledston Hall is visible half right in the distance) and under a conveyor belt which crosses the river. When the fence turns sharp left, keep with it, and here in front is the old River Aire, which comes to a sudden end at this point.

Pass through a kissing-gate, with Lowther Lake ahead, and keep on by the high fence until it turns sharp left uphill with an enclosed path beside it: here keep forward with a hedge/fence to your left and the lake still to your right. When the hedge ends, go through the gap by the gate and follow the track up to a cross path at the top, turn right, ignore a gate on the left leading into a fenced path and keep forward with a fence to your left. The path becomes enclosed and crosses a footbridge before reaching the old river bank. Turn left through the kissing-gate and along the flood bank. There are extensive wetlands to the left. Soon you join the new cut near its end. Follow the high flood bank until it curves left, then keep forward over a stile and along a lower flood bank.

Cross another stile and walk along the river bank to the next facing fence, where a painted arrow directs you left to a gate out onto the road in Allerton Bywater opposite the Victoria Hotel. Turn right along the road. Along the first street on the left, opposite the telephone kiosk, is another pub, The Anchor. Having passed the line of the old railway, now being planted with trees and landscaped, keep right at the fork, along a road which ends at yet another pub, The Boat. The footpath passes to the right of the pub and becomes a paved path by the river. As one walks along there is another fine view of Ledston Hall to the left. When the paved path ends leave the river and keep forward along the track to the A656. Keep straight forward into Castleford. Cross the canal and some distance further on Castleford Bridge over the Aire and turn right past The Ship along Aire Street. Opposite Allinson's flour mill cross the road at the traffic lights and walk up to the right of the Job Centre. At the next main road turn right and walk along as far as Powell Street on the left. This leads to the station.

USEFUL ADDRESSES

Ramblers' Association (West Riding Area):
Area Secretary,
25 Rossett Beck, Harrogate HG2 9NT (tel: 01423-872268).
Publications Section,
27 Cookridge Avenue, Leeds LS16 7NA (tel: 0113-267-4797).
Ramblers' Association Central Office,
1-5 Wandsworth Road, London SW8 2XX (tel: 0171-582-6878).
National Trust, Malham Tarn Estate Office,
Malham Tarn, Settle, North Yorkshire BD24 9PT (tel: 01729-830416).
Eye on the Aire (a voluntary association set up in 1988 to promote the environmental improvement of the River Aire on its 21 mile journey from Apperley Bridge to Castleford),
74 Kirkgate, Leeds LS2 7DJ (tel: 0113-234-6223).

Path problems should be reported to:
(Between Castleford and Apperley Bridge)
Leeds Leisure Services, Countryside Service, Rights of Way Section, Red Hall, Red Hall Lane, Leeds LS17 8NB.
(Between Apperley Bridge and Steeton)
Bradford Metropolitan District Public Rights of Way Section, Holycroft, Goulbourne Street, Keighley BD21 1PY (tel: 01535-618300).
(Between Steeton and Bell Busk)
North Yorkshire County Council, Skipton Area Office, Public Rights of Way Section, Croft House, Carleton Road, Skipton, North Yorkshire BD23 2BG (tel: 01756-793344).
(Between Bell Busk and Malham Tarn)
Yorkshire Dales National Park, South West Area Office, Stone Dykes Barn, Stainforth, Settle, North Yorkshire BD24 9PN (tel: 01729-822293).

Tourist Information Centres:
Gateway Yorkshire,
Leeds City Station, Leeds LS1 1PL (tel: 0113-242-5242).
Skipton TIC,
9 Sheep Street, Skipton BD23 1JH (tel: 01756-792809).
National Park Centre, Malham, via Skipton,
North Yorkshire BD23 4DA (tel: 01729-830363).

RECORD OF THE AIREDALE WAY

Date	Place	Km	Km Total	Start Time	Finish Time	Comments
	Leeds Station	0	0			
	Newlay Bridge	7.8	7.8			
	Leeds Ring Road	2.0	9.8			
	Apperley Bridge	3.7	13.5			
	Esholt village	4.5	18.0			
	Shipley Bridge	4.2	22.2			
	Saltaire	1.2	23.4			

	Bingley Bridge	6.3	29.7		
	Marley	2.2	31.9		
	Aire Br., Keighley	3.6	35.5		
	Low Utley	2.4	37.9		
	Silsden Bridge	3.4	41.3		
	Kildwick Bridge	3.0	44.3		
	Cononley Bridge	3.6	47.9		
	Carleton Bridge	4.7	52.6		
	Skipton Station	1.8	54.4		

A59	Gargrave Bridge	Coniston Cold	Bell Busk	Airton Bridge	Hanlith	Malham	Malham Tarn
2.7	4.3	3.4	1.3	4.1	2.0	1.8	4.5
57.1	61.4	64.8	66.1	70.2	72.2	74.0	78.5

RECORD OF WALKS COMPLETED

Date	Walk	Start Time	Finish Time	Comments
⟵⎯⎯⎯⟶	Leeds-Horsforth			
	Horsforth-Apperley Bridge			
SUN 06/02/05	Apperley Bridge-Shipley	11 AM	4 PM	50MIN 'DETOUR' + 40MINS REST PRETTY UGLY SCENERY!
	Shipley-Bingley			
	Bingley-Keighley			
	Keighley-Steeton			
	Cross Hills-Pinnacles			
	Steeton-Cononley			

	Kildwick-Jubilee Tower	Cononley-Lothersdale	Cononley-Skipton	Low Bradley	Carleton Glen	Skipton-Sharp Haw	Skipton-Gargrave	Gargrave-Airton	Airton-Malham Tarn	Down River